LINCOLN CHRISTIAN COLLEGE

P9-CCS-446

OLD TESTAMENT GUIDES

General Editor

R.N. Whybray

HAGGAI, ZECHARIAH, MALACHI

Other titles in this series include

THE SECOND ISAIAH
R.N. Whybray

1 AND 2 SAMUEL
R.P. Gordon

JUDGES
A.D.H. Mayes

DANIEL
P.R. Davies

JOB
J.H. Eaton

AMOS
A.G. Auld

EZRA AND NEHEMIAH
H.G.M. Williamson

HAGGAI
ZECHARIAH
MALACHI

R.J. Coggins

Published by JSOT Press
for the Society for Old Testament Study

Copyright © 1987 Sheffield Academic Press

Published by JSOT Press
JSOT Press is an imprint of
Sheffield Academic Press
The University of Sheffield
343 Fulwood Road
Sheffield S10 3BP
England

Typeset by Sheffield Academic Press
and
printed in Great Britain
by Billings & Sons Ltd
Worcester

British Library Cataloguing in Publication Data

Coggins, R.J.
    Haggai, Zechariah, Malachi.—(Old
    Testament guides, ISSN 0264-6498)
    1. Bible. O.T. Haggai—Commentaries
    2. Bible. O.T. Zechariah—Commentaries
    I. Title   II. Society for Old Testament
                        Study

    III. Series
    224'.9707   BS1655.3

    ISBN 1-85075-025-4

CONTENTS

74842

ABBREVIATIONS

ANET	*Ancient Near Eastern Texts Relating to the Old Testament*, ed. J.B. Pritchard, Princeton: Princeton University Press, 3rd edn, 1969
BH	*Biblia Hebraica*, ed. R. Kittel, 7th edn, Stuttgart: Württembergische Bibelanstalt, 1951
BHS	*Biblia Hebraica Stuttgartensia*, ed. K. Elliger and W. Rudolph, Stuttgart: Deutsche Bibelstiftung, 1977
BJRL	*Bulletin of the John Rylands Library*
CBC	*Cambridge Bible Commentary*
CBQ	*Catholic Biblical Quarterly*
DOTT	*Documents from Old Testament Times*, ed. D.W. Thomas, London: Nelson, 1958
ExpT	*Expository Times*
IB	*The Interpreter's Bible*
ICC	International Critical Commentary
IDB	*The Interpreter's Dictionary of the Bible*
IDB(S)	*The Interpreter's Dictionary of the Bible*, Supplementary Volume
JNES	*Journal of Near Eastern Studies*
JSOT	*Journal for the Study of the Old Testament*
KAT	Kommentar zum Alten Testament
NEB	*New English Bible*
OTL	Old Testament Library
RSV	Revised Standard Version
RV	Revised Version
SVT	Supplements to *Vetus Testamentum*
TBC	Torch Bible Commentaries
TOTC	Tyndale Old Testament Commentaries
VT	*Vetus Testamentum*
WBC	Word Biblical Commentary
ZAW	*Zeitschrift für die alttestamentliche Wissenschaft*
ZThK	*Zeitschrift für Theologie und Kirche*

1

THE
HISTORICAL
SETTING

The Persians

DURING THE YEARS from 558 to 529 BC Cyrus, king of Anshan, an otherwise almost unknown area in ancient Elam and now part of modern Iran, east of the Persian Gulf, engaged in a series of conquests. The Babylonian Empire, which had up to that time controlled the Tigris-Euphrates basin, often called Mesopotamia, was overthrown, and Babylon itself captured. A new power was established, now generally known as the Persian Empire, whose western boundaries extended into modern Turkey and reached to the borders of Egypt. (In the fifth century BC the Persians were to attempt to extend their power still further west, into the area of modern Europe, by the conquest of some of the Greek city-states.) Those parts of the texts with which this book is concerned which can be dated—that is, Haggai and Zechariah 1–8—come from this period when Persian rule was first being established in Syria-Palestine.

Persian rule was to last for some two hundred years, until the conquests of Alexander the Great about 330 BC; yet our knowledge both of the Persian Empire in general and of its impact in Syria-Palestine in particular remains very limited. The Old Testament is in fact one of our chief sources of information; yet, by comparison with the Assyrians and Babylonians of an earlier period, our references are few, even though Persian rule lasted for so much longer. Nor is there from Persian sources anything comparable to the wealth of Assyrian and Babylonian inscriptional material which has been excavated within the last century. (The most important exception to this is the 'Cyrus Cylinder', now in the British Museum in London, which relates to the conquest of Babylon.)

To a large extent our knowledge of the Persian Empire depends on two kinds of literary source: the Hebrew Bible—our Old Testament—and a variety of classical Greek authors. The impressions that we gain from these two sources are markedly different. For the Greeks, the Persians embodied the threat of tyranny. They were despised as Asiatic barbarians and also feared as liable to overthrow all that the Greeks held most dear. Those whose knowledge of the Persians is derived from classical sources, in particular Herodotus' *History*, with its description of Leonidas's gallant resistance at Thermopylae, or the naval battle at Salamis, may tend instinctively to regard them as an alien force, an oppressor posing a threat to the very survival of civilization. (In fairness, it must be said that this attitude to the Persians was not universal among Greek writers, especially those from a slightly later age: Xenophon's *Anabasis* [the *Persian Expedition* as it is usually called in translation], which was written in the changed historical circumstances of the fourth century BC, is remarkably sympathetic towards them.)

From the various Old Testament sources a very different picture emerges. Cyrus himself is described in the book of Isaiah as 'the shepherd' and 'the anointed' of Yahweh the god of Israel (Isa.44.28; 45.1); much of the book of Ezra is given over to an account of the favourable treatment of the Jews by Persian rulers; Nehemiah combined the roles of leadership of the Jewish community and personal attendance (conventionally that of 'cup-bearer') upon the Persian king; and (whatever may be thought of the historicity of the events concerned) both the story of Esther and the episode of Daniel in the lions' den (Dan. 6) picture Persian emperors in highly favourable terms. The books of Haggai and Zechariah are less specific, but there too the opening verses seem to share the same spirit. Each of these books is dated by the years of the reign of the Persian emperor Darius, as if his rule were part of the divine ordering of affairs. It is striking that in Haggai (1.1, 15) Darius is simply called 'the king'. One can scarcely imagine the words of pre-exilic prophets being dated by the years of rule of an Assyrian king.

No attempt will be made here to assess whether the Greek or the Israelite view was a more accurate reflection of the 'reality' of the Persian Empire and its rule of subject people. To attempt to do so would be to suppose that rulers can be labelled good or bad according to some pre-determined set of criteria. (This point needs to be made, for only too often the religious assessments of the Deuteronomistic editors of the Books of Kings are carried over into historical treatments as if they could be regarded as objective historical judgments.)

The fact remains—and this is extremely important for our understanding—that the Old Testament gives a consistently favourable view of Persian rule, even though the continuance of that rule meant a loss of independence for the people of Israel. Why this should be so remains uncertain, though some possible contributory factors can be discerned. One such cause—which should not be dismissed as mere cynicism—may well be the fact that much of the Old Testament reached its final form during the period of Persian dominance, and so will naturally have reflected the political realities of the time of its final redaction. Another may be the fact that the Persians, unlike the Assyrians and the Babylonians, had made no direct attack upon Israel or Judah; there was no such traumatic experience as the destruction of Jerusalem and its temple in 587/6 to be associated with them. It is also possible (though this is much disputed) that the official Persian religion, Zoroastrianism, came to be regarded by the Jews as less incompatible with the worship of Yahweh than were the religious systems of earlier conquerors. However this may be, one aspect of Persian religious policy will certainly have been very acceptable to the religious leaders of the Jewish community: the Persians seem deliberately to have encouraged local cults as a way of promoting loyalty within the empire and of maintaining its cohesion. Local shrines were built or rebuilt, their worship was promoted with state subsidies, and a sympathetic attitude was adopted towards the diversities of religious observance of the subject peoples.

'Pre-Exilic' and 'Post-Exilic'

Comparison of the Persians with the Assyrians and the Babylonians should warn us against another assumption which is common in Old Testament study. It is conventional to divide the material into 'pre-exilic' and 'post-exilic', as if the two periods could be sharply differentiated from one another. It is of course true that the absorption of Judah into the Babylonian Empire from 597, the destruction of Jerusalem in 587/6 and the exile of many leading citizens were all deeply disturbing experiences which left a profound and lasting imprint on the community. But we need also to remember that the human instinct for continuity is a very strong one; that life will have continued in Judah and Jerusalem even when many were exiled (and even though the Bible tells us little about such life). Indeed, as we shall see, one legitimate interpretation of the message of Haggai is that it is a plea for 'business as usual'.

The expression 'post-exilic period' also contains an ambiguity: what do we mean by 'the exile', and how should it be dated? Even with regard to the date when it began there are some problems, though these, which arise from the incomplete nature of our evidence, may be regarded as mere matters of detail. The idea of an 'end' of the exile, however, poses much greater difficulties. If we accept Ezra 1–3 as a straightforward historical record, the picture we shall have is of a mass return from Babylon to Judah in or about 538, so that it becomes possible to speak as if the exile were now over. There are, however, a number of pointers which suggest that such a view is dangerously over-simplified. There is evidence of a continuing established community of Jews in Babylon (the fifth-century Marashu Tablets: *DOTT*, 95f.; *ANET*, 221f.); it is clear both from the Cyrus Cylinder (*DOTT*, 92–94; *ANET*, 315) and from the Aramaic form of the decree allowing the rebuilding of the Jerusalem temple (Ezra 6.3-5) that Cyrus's policy was much more a matter of the re-establishment of local cults than of a mass return of exiles; and it is very probable that the book of Ezra, which is our only source suggesting a mass return, had a particular polemical purpose: to stress the loyalty and obedience of the community which had gone through the purifying experience of exile over against the suspect motives of those who had remained in Palestine, who were no better than 'the adversaries of Judah and Benjamin' (Ezra 4.1).

When we turn to Haggai and Zechariah, we find no indication that these prophets thought of themselves as living in an era that was in some way marked off as decisively different from that of their predecessors. We shall be wise to avoid labelling these prophets as 'post-exilic', if by that we intend to imply that some barrier divided them from all that had gone before. In many respects we should obtain a more instructive picture if we envisaged all the prophets whose words have been set down and recorded in distinct books as having lived during the period when Israel and Judah were under threat from, or actually subservient to, various great empires—Assyria, Babylon, Persia. (It will be noted that so far no reference has been made to Malachi, for the good reason that we have no clear evidence about the historical background of that book. If the commonly held view is correct that it dates from the first half of the fifth century, the same considerations would apply as for Haggai and Zechariah; but this cannot be firmly established. See Chapter 8 below.)

The Immediate Background

The general historical setting of the ministry of Haggai and Zechariah is, therefore, established beyond reasonable doubt. They lived and proclaimed the word of Yahweh at the time when Persian rule in Palestine was being established, and the immediate impression which they give is that they were in no way opposed in principle to the establishment of that rule. When we come to look at the historical situation in greater detail, however, certain problems arise.

Cyrus, the founder of the Persian Empire, died in 529 and was succeeded by his son Cambyses (529-522). Under his rule Persian power was extended to the borders of Egypt, and it may well be that it was only under Cambyses that Persian control over Palestine was effectively established. If this were so (and the evidence is ambiguous) problems for Old Testament interpretation would obviously arise; but since these are more relevant to the book of Ezra than to Haggai and Zechariah they will not be pursued here. What is clear is, first, that Cambyses was master of Palestine and intended it as the base for his attempt to invade Egypt about 525, and secondly that his death in 522 precipitated a series of riots which put the whole empire under pressure for more than a year. Eventually Darius I Hystaspes established himself as king (522/1-486), and, as we have already seen, Haggai and Zechariah 1-8 are dated in relation to his reign.

Attempts have been made to relate the ministry of these two prophets in a precise way to the various disturbances which preceded the establishment of Darius on the throne. Particular significance has been seen in the alleged 'disappearance' of Zerubbabel, the community leader who is prominent in Haggai but is mentioned much more obliquely in Zechariah and then seems not to have been involved in any subsequent events. There have been attempts to picture the Jewish leaders as engaging in conspiracy against the Persian government, for example that of L. Waterman ('The Camouflaged Purge of Three Messianic Conspirators', *JNES* 13

[1954], 73ff.), who attempted to establish a precise series of cross-references between the hopes expressed in Haggai and Zechariah and the political situation of the time. But where much remains unknown such neat and tidy correlations must always remain suspect, and there seems little in the books of Haggai and Zechariah as they have come down to us to suggest that these prophets had a primary political or anti-Persian concern. The most that we can say is that in general terms the widespread political upheavals of 522/1 may have provided part of the occasion for the prophetic word: an appropriate opportunity to recall the community to their basic priorities.

Darius, then, was established in control of the Empire, and it is clear that permission was available for the rebuilding of the Jerusalem temple. (Ezra 5–6 supplies a fuller account of the course of events. As we have already noted, historical problems abound when the book of Ezra is our only source; nevertheless it is often held that these chapters, written in Aramaic, provide a basically reliable report of the main developments.) With regard to Haggai in particular, one of the main themes of that prophet's message was a summons to the people to address themselves to the work on the temple: 1.1–2.9 and 2.15-19 are largely devoted to this.

But an historical difficulty arises straightaway. According to Ezra 3, a start on the work of rebuilding had already been made in 538, immediately upon the first return of exiles from Babylon; yet Hag. 1.4, 9 speak of 'the house', that is, the temple, lying in ruins. Apparently, according to this, no work of rebuilding had yet been done. It would obviously be possible to construct some kind of harmonization of the two accounts: one might argue that work done nearly twenty years before Haggai's time and then neglected would now be in ruins. Alternatively, there is a possibility that the verb *yasad*, habitually translated 'lay foundations' (Hag. 2.18; Zech. 4.9; 8.9), has a broader and less specific sense, so that it might refer to any kind of repair work (so A. Gelston, 'The Foundations of the Second Temple' *VT* 16 [1966], 232-35; J.G. Baldwin, *Haggai, Zechariah, Malachi*, 52f. [see the bibliography to ch. 4]). Opinions will differ about the plausibility of such an approach; the view taken here is that it is more realistic to recognize different viewpoints in the two books, with Ezra anxious to stress the devotedness of the returned exiles (whose numbers were, according to Ezra 2, very considerable), and Haggai more concerned to draw attention to the lack of any real progress in the rebuilding of the temple. Historically, the contemporary report in Haggai is likely to be the more accurate, but that should not be the only criterion of judgment. Just as the writer of Ezra was anxious to stress how God's favour had induced loyalty in the community, so it was important for Haggai to emphasize how much more needed to be done.

Whether or not some preliminary work on the temple had been done, there was still much to be achieved, and this was a major focus of Haggai's prophetic words. Some indeed have argued that it was his main or even sole concern; but that issue can be deferred until Chapter 4. For the moment we must attend to the other major historical problem which arises. This concerns the leaders of the Jerusalem community.

With regard to Joshua all is reasonably clear. His name, although spelt Joshua in Haggai and Zechariah and Jeshua in Ezra and Nehemiah, presents no problem: there is no doubt that the same person is meant. Possibly the form with an 'e' arose because the two vowels 'o' and 'u' were not acceptable in later Hebrew in adjacent positions (so Rudolph, *Haggai, Sacharja 1–8, Sacharja 9–14, Maleachi* [KAT XIII/4], 31). Certainly such a vowel-shift became customary: thus the Greek form of the name is 'Jesus'.

In Haggai Joshua is regularly referred to as 'the high priest'. (There must presumably have been a chief or leading priest in the pre-exilic Jerusalem temple; but Joshua may have been the first to hold high-priestly office in the full ritual sense described in the books of Exodus to Numbers.) There is, however, one respect in which the books of Haggai and Zechariah differ in their presentation of Joshua: in Haggai he is mentioned only together with Zerubbabel, whereas in Zechariah he plays the more important role of the two. It has often been concluded from this that Zerubbabel had for some reason been removed from the scene, leaving the Jerusalem community from this time until the second century BC without a 'secular' leader, or at least one descended from the Davidic line. That is to say, the high priest now became in effect the sole leader of the community.

This development did in fact take place, but only at a time later than that of Haggai and Zechariah. Haggai, at least, regarded Zerubbabel as the 'governor' (1.1 and elsewhere); that is, as the chief secular authority. The main historical problem regarding the leadership of the community is thus that of the fate of Zerubbabel. On this question many scholars have maintained that the relative silence of Zechariah concerning Zerubbabel is due simply to the particular interests of that book and not to some more sinister cause. So P.R. Ackroyd speaks of 'some extravagant theories about the fate which he (Zerubbabel) met at the hands of the Persians' (*Exile and Restoration*, 147). (The most acute historical problem concerning Zerubbabel arises, however, not in connection with the books of Haggai and Zechariah but with the early chapters of Ezra. There the difficult question of the relation of Zerubbabel to one Sheshbazzar, described in Ezra 5.16 as the one who 'laid the foundations of the house of God', is also involved. Sheshbazzar is not mentioned at all in Haggai or Zechariah.)

The problem—as far as the books of Haggai and Zechariah are concerned—centres upon Zech. 6.9ff., where it has often been maintained that the present form of the text has undergone modification. This view arises from the fact that in both vv. 11 and 14 the Hebrew text has 'crowns'. This is the translation found in RV, but most modern translations have an emendation to the singular 'crown'. (This is what is found in RSV, where the margin notes that the Hebrew word is plural in form.) An explanation of this difficulty, which has been described in one of the most recent commentaries (Amsler on Haggai, in S. Amsler, A. Lacocque and R. Vuilleumier, *Aggée, Zacharie, Malachie* [Commentaire de l'Ancien Testament XIc], Geneva: Labor et Fides, 1981, 108) as 'the classical hypothesis' concerning this section, is that a reference to Zerubbabel originally stood in the text at this point, but was removed by an ancient redactor after the disappearance of Zerubbabel from the scene. This theory dates back at least to the time of Wellhausen in the later nineteenth century and has been widely followed more recently. It is an ingenious theory, though in view of the evidence of later editorial work on the book (see ch. 3 below) it must remain doubtful whether so neat a solution is wholly plausible. (See p. 47 for a further discussion of this section.)

It is wise, therefore, to be cautious about supposing that the apparent 'playing down' of Zerubbabel is of particular significance. In any case it is important not to allow the historical setting to be the only determining factor in the understanding of these prophets. It is clear that for the author of Ezra the particular importance of Haggai and Zechariah was their role in the rebuilding of the temple. For him this and the establishment of the temple ritual were of supreme importance, and the prophetic figures of that period *must* have had as their principal purpose the encouragement of the people in the fulfilment of that task.

When we come to look more closely at the books of Haggai and Zechariah 1–8, however, we receive a somewhat different impression. Undeniably the little book of Haggai is much concerned with the rebuilding of the temple: 1.1–2.9 deal with practically nothing else. But whereas in Ezra it seems almost as though the rebuilding of the temple was a sufficient end in itself, in Haggai the temple is important as a vital means to the end of establishing the standing of the community before its God, so that the 'shaking of the heavens and the earth' of which 2.21 speaks might begin. We shall return in Chapter 4 to the interpretation of this difficult phrase, and in Chapter 5 to the more extensive material in Zechariah which also regards the rebuilding of the temple as no more than an essential preliminary to the great events which he expected to come about. For the present we may simply be content to bear in mind that for these, as for the other prophets of Israel, the particular historical circumstances of their time were no more than the incidental background to their belief in God and his direction of human affairs.

In historical terms it must appear that the expectations of these prophets were disappointed. We know that the temple was rebuilt, and was completed and dedicated in the sixth year of Darius, that is 516/5 (Ezra 6.14–16). Thus began what Jewish writers habitually call the Second Temple period. Of historical events affecting the Jerusalem community in following generations we know nothing. The book of Ezra passes over a gap of some 60 years—longer if Ezra's own mission is dated later than that of Nehemiah—effectively in silence, with nothing more than an 'after this' (Ezra 7.1). Persian rule, once established, was not to come under serious threat as far as Palestine was concerned until the rise of Alexander the Great in the 330s. If Haggai and Zechariah had expected that the turn of historical events would produce some dramatic change of fortune for their community they were disappointed. But we should be cautious about assuming that they were simply mistaken: had that been so, it is scarcely likely that their words would have been treasured and preserved and shaped into the books which we now have. In some sense at least these men were perceived as having carried out a true prophetic role. It is to the nature of that prophetic ministry that we must now turn.

Further Reading

The standard histories of Israel all give clear and adequate accounts of the period and of the affairs of the Jerusalem community. They have in common a tendency to accept uncritically the favourable view of Persian rule presented by the biblical material, and also, in varying degrees, a tendency to accept the evidence of Haggai and Zechariah 1–8 rather than that of Ezra 1–6 in reconstructing the history of the period. Among the standard histories the following may be mentioned:

M. Noth, *The History of Israel*, London: A. & C. Black, 1958 (reissued, SCM Press, 1984), 305-15.

J. Bright, *A History of Israel*, London: SCM Press, 1960 and subsequent editions, 344-55.

S. Herrmann, *A History of Israel in Old Testament Times*, London: SCM Press, 1975, 298-306. (This deals more specifically than Noth or Bright with the problems arising from the differences between Ezra and Haggai–Zechariah.)

J.A. Soggin, *A History of Israel*, London: SCM Press, 1984, 261-72. (This also includes detailed bibliography of other relevant books and articles.)

Among more detailed studies may be noted:

R.S. Foster, *The Restoration of Israel*, London: Darton, Longman & Todd, 1970, 144-60. (Readable, but now somewhat dated.)

P.R. Ackroyd, *Exile and Restoration*, London: SCM Press, 1968, 38-52. (The whole book, which is sub-titled 'A Study of Hebrew Thought of the Sixth Century BC', contains much that is relevant to this study.)

J.H. Hayes & J.M. Miller (eds.), *Israelite and Judaean History*, London: SCM Press, 1977, especially 515-23. (In this very detailed study of the problems of the historical setting of the Old Testament material, the whole of ch. IX, 'The Persian Period' by G. Widengren (489-538) contains relevant material and full bibliographies.)

W.D. Davies & J. Finkelstein (eds.), *The Cambridge History of Judaism*, I, Cambridge: Cambridge University Press, 1984, ch. 7, especially 135-41.

2

PROPHETS UNDER
ALIEN RULE

ANY DISCUSSION of the role of prophets in the Old Testament needs to begin by making as clear as possible what is being discussed. In contemporary English the word 'prophet' may be used in a general sense of one who foretells the future, and the adjective 'prophetic' can function as an appropriate designation of someone who appears to be gifted with insight: with the ability to discern the complexities of a situation in a way not given to lesser individuals. On the other hand, there is a specialized use of the term which refers to a particular part of the Hebrew Bible as 'the Prophets': Joshua–2 Kings as 'the Former Prophets' and Isaiah, Jeremiah, Ezekiel and the twelve Minor Prophets collectively as 'the Latter Prophets'.

Although Haggai, Zechariah and Malachi fall within this last group, it is with none of these descriptions that we are here primarily concerned. Rather, our starting-point should be the existence among the important religious personnel of ancient Israel, alongside priests, doorkeepers, singers and the like, of a group known as $n^e bi'im$, a word which is regularly translated 'prophets' in modern versions of the Bible. However, although there are many references to $n^e bi'im$ in the Old Testament, there is still much about these men and women which remains in dispute. (Coggins, Phillips and Knibb, eds., *Israel's Prophetic Tradition*, 1982, provides a full survey of recent scholarly work on the prophets; J. Blenkinsopp, *A History of Prophecy in Israel*, 1984, is an attempt to trace the development of the institution which, unlike many other such studies, takes seriously the place of prophets in the period with which we are concerned. In addition, there is a vast secondary literature on all aspects of the prophets and prophetism.)

Our immediate concern is a more limited one: an attempt to identify the particular role of Haggai and Zechariah. Now in using the word 'role' we have already implied a particular understanding of the prophets. The Old Testament prophets have often been regarded as a varied group united by nothing more than the fact that each was in his own unique way commissioned by God to proclaim a message to the people. If that were the whole of the story, no search for a human 'role' would be profitable: their 'role' would be hidden in the providence of God. But whatever one's views may be about the prophets as proclaimers of divine truths (for not all who study their writings will themselves be believers), it is legitimate and valuable to attempt to discover the actual place in society occupied by prophets, and, having done that, to see how Haggai and Zechariah fitted into that role.

It has often been noted that the ministry of many—perhaps all—of the prophets was exercised in relation to court and cult. Prophets could be bitterly critical of kings and their policies, and could attack the cultic practice of their day; but the criticisms are, as it were, from within. It appears as if it were the role of the prophet on the one hand to ensure that the king maintained a policy consistent with loyalty to Yahweh, and on the other to insist that the cult, the place where Yahweh's holiness was especially to be manifested, must be a worthy vehicle for that manifestation.

If this is a correct understanding of the role of prophets, what became of the institution of prophetism when there was no longer a king and the cult was in disarray? On the one hand it may be no coincidence that we hear nothing about prophets working in Judah during the half-century following the destruction of the temple and the ending of Judah's independent existence as a state. On the other, with regard to the prophets in exile in Babylon during that period, it is noteworthy that the old concerns persisted. Ezekiel's oracles are regularly dated according to the years of the exiled king Jehoiachin, and his concern for the Jerusalem cult is of paramount importance throughout that book; while the other prophetic material from a Babylonian setting, Isaiah 40–55, is significantly not associated with a named prophet but forms part of a larger collection of prophetic material which is also characterized by strong royal and cultic concerns.

By 520 or thereabouts, however, significant changes had taken place. The old concerns of cult and court could once again come to the fore in a direct manner, and the possibility of prophetic ministry in its traditional context was once again a real one. Yet the circumstances were in many respects drastically changed. With Haggai and Zechariah the prophetic ministry was still characteristically linked with court and cult, but in a markedly different way. The attacks of Amos on Jeroboam II (Amos 7) and of Isaiah on Ahaz (Isaiah 7) and the sweeping condemnations of Hosea and Micah against all the royal establishment of their day find no echo here. On the contrary, Haggai and Zechariah saw as one of their primary tasks the establishment of a true court. Whatever else may need to be said about the final verses in Haggai (2.20-23), the emphasis in this passage on the chosen status of the Davidic descendant Zerubbabel is one point that we must bear in mind. Not to condemn the contemporary court, but to play a part in its re-founding, was the role of these prophets.

Similar considerations apply when we turn to the attitude of the prophets to the cult. Here again, before the exile condemnation had been drastic. We must of course be wary of treating the prophets of Israel as if they were Liberal Protestants born out of due time, who supposed that all forms of cultic worship were mere optional, and perhaps not even desirable, extras to some inner perception of the fatherhood of God and the brotherhood of man. It is rather the case that the eighth-century prophets had condemned the cult *of their own day* as totally unacceptable, at least partly because what should have been the chief means of communication between God and his worshippers had been corrupted. (Amos 5.18ff.; Hos. 6.6; Isa. 1.10ff.; and Mic. 6.6-8 are among the most familiar of the many passages of condemnation.) In Haggai and Zechariah we find the same concern with the importance of cult, but this is now expressed from a very different point of view. The condemnation of the community is now based on cultic abuse of quite another kind—the failure to re-establish the regular cultic round in the temple. Only when that has been done can there by any hope of the return of divine favour (Hag. 1.7-11).

There is one passage in these prophetic collections which at first glance appears to follow the earlier line of condemnation but is actually significantly different. Mal. 1.6-10 is sharply condemnatory of the sacrificial offerings being made at 'the LORD's table', in a manner which is at first sight reminiscent of the attacks of the eighth-century prophets. But in fact the reason for this attack is very different. Here the people, and more specifically the priests, are condemned because they attempt to evade their responsibilities by offering to God in sacrifice imperfect victims of a kind they would never dare to bring to the (Persian) governor (1.8; it is not explicitly stated, but seems very likely, that the 'governor' referred to here was the Persian imperial representative). This is in complete contrast to the pre-exilic prophets, who never condemned priests or people on grounds such as these: if anything, they tended to warn their audiences against supposing that an over-eager fulfilling of religious duties was itself a good thing (cf. the irony of Amos 4.4f.).

There is, then, some evidence to support the view that prophetism as a religious institution was bound up with a particular set of social circumstances which were for all practical purposes those of the monarchical period. Seen thus, Haggai and Zechariah represent a late flowering of the phenomenon of prophetism, from a period when hopes were high that something of former glories could be achieved once more. (This thesis concerning prophetism in general has been advanced by various scholars in recent years: see especially F.M. Cross, *Canaanite Myth and Hebrew Epic*, 223, for a concise statement. Fuller discussion will be found in D.L. Petersen, *Late Israelite Prophecy*, ch. 1, and in P.D. Hanson, *The Dawn of Apocalyptic*—see especially the Excursus, 'The History of Prophecy in Israel', 12-16. Hanson's work will be discussed more fully with reference to its presentation of Haggai and Zechariah in Chapter 6.)

An approach of this kind, linking prophets with court and cult, even to the extent (in Hanson, quoted by Petersen, *op. cit.*, 6) of comparing the prophet with the court vizier, is certainly welcome in so far as it takes seriously the question of the sociological status of prophets. Too often they have been treated as *sui generis*, a group of holy men whose role bore no relation to the norms of the society of their day. If it is possible to identify their role more precisely, the potential gain in our understanding of the world of ancient Israel is considerable.

Nevertheless, before we simply accept the view that Haggai and Zechariah, and other prophets before them, confirm the dictum that 'the locus of classical Israelite prophecy was the institution of monarchy' (Petersen, 3), we should note a number of questions which need to be raised about such a reconstruction.

(1) First, it runs counter to much recent emphasis on the prophetic

message as primary and information about the *messenger* as never more than secondary and incidental. It must be asked in relation to *all* the prophetic collections whether the literature in the form in which it has come down to us allows us to draw detailed conclusions concerning the social role of Israel's prophets.

(2) Secondly, it must be recognized that our knowledge of the role of Haggai and Zechariah is even slighter than that which is available for earlier prophets. For all practical purposes we are totally dependent upon the books named after them, and very different conclusions have been drawn from these concerning the precise ministry which the prophets exercised as individuals.

(3) Thirdly, and more specifically, while in the case of Haggai it is possible to make out a plausible case for seeing him as pleading for a restoration of both court and cult, such a view is much more difficult to sustain with regard to Zechariah. Only by emending Zech. 6.9-15 so as to introduce a reference to Zerubbabel where none exists in the present Hebrew text is it possible to see any significant 'courtly' concern in his book.

(4) A fourth difficulty with regard to the theory just outlined is of a somewhat different kind. It concerns two passages in Zechariah which refer to prophets and prophecy. These are very different in character. In Zech. 1.3-6 allusion is made to 'the former prophets'. This should not be taken as referring to 'the Former Prophets' in the sense in which that expression is used to describe a part of the Hebrew Bible. It simply means prophets of earlier times, envisaged as God's messengers to his people, who had pronounced words of warning which had been ignored until the threats contained in them had materialized. This passage comes from the editorial framework to Zechariah (see Chapter 3), and suggests that, at least for those who gathered together the oracles of Zechariah, there was already a body of tradition available which could be described as 'the former prophets'. In the context of these verses, Zechariah's own position seems to be somewhat ambiguous: he is himself described as a prophet (1.1) who is reiterating the message of the former prophets, yet he is also to be differentiated from them, since they are pictured as a group from an earlier age (v. 5). This section may, therefore, hint at a shift in the meaning of 'prophet', from being a term denoting a group with a particular social role to one which was associated with a body of written material. (See on this R.A. Mason, 'The Purpose of the "Editorial Framework" of the Book of Haggai', *VT* 27 [1977], 413-21.)

The other reference to prophets in Zechariah is in 13.2-6. (In the discussion so far it has been assumed that Zechariah 9-14 are to be sharply distinguished from chs. 1-8. This is the view taken by almost all modern commentators, though a partial exception is provided by J.G. Baldwin. See Chapters 3 and 7 below for fuller discussion of this point. What all commentators agree upon is the extreme difficulty of establishing the date and original setting of chs. 9-14.) Of many difficult passages in chs. 9-14, 13.2-6 is one of the most controversial. One possible interpretation is to suppose, as do Hanson (367) and Lacocque (194-95), that the reference here is to *false* prophets, whose corruption is denounced. But such an interpretation, though it eases the difficulties of exegesis, raises an ambiguity. At one level it is clear that those being denounced are regarded as false: that is why they are being condemned. But it is very difficult to see any grounds in this passage for supposing that a distinction is made between the group of prophets which is condemned and some other group of 'true' prophets. Nowhere, for example, is prophetic status claimed for the author of Zech. 9-14. The simpler interpretation of this passage is therefore more probably the right one: that prophetism as an institution has fallen into disrepute, and all who claim that title are rejected (so, among many commentators, Mason: see the bibliography to Chapter 4).

Clearly it would be unwise to attempt to draw precise conclusions from so difficult a passage as this, but at least it must raise questions concerning a necessary link between prophetism and the court as its setting. Rather, it would seem that the office of prophet did continue in some circles after the time of Joshua and Zerubbabel, but that it fell into disrepute for reasons which we cannot now identify. If this is so, then we are warned against any attempt to link prophetism too specifically with the monarchical period.

There is a further implication of this which should be noted. The relation of prophets to politics has been much discussed. Isaiah of Jerusalem, for example, has sometimes been seen very much as a political figure, advising the king and his counsellors about the most appropriate course of action in the face of threats from Judah's northern neighbours or from the Assyrians. In contrast, it has sometimes been argued that such a presentation of Isaiah is quite misleading: his pleas for simple trust in Yahweh's guidance (e.g. Isa. 30.15a) represent a *rejection* of any political involvement. There is a similar ambiguity with regard to the possible political stance of

Haggai and Zechariah 1-8, though this has received much less attention. On the one hand, it could be argued that, since religion and politics were inextricably tied together in the ancient world, both Haggai's concern for the speedy restoration of the Jerusalem temple and his oracles addressed to Zerubbabel were essentially political. On that view, the underlying thrust of Haggai's words would be his judgment that the upheavals currently affecting the Persian Empire were such that it was important for the Jewish community to be prepared for the opportunity to restore its political fortunes and once more become an independent state. The temple would then have been regarded by Haggai and his hearers as a focus of national and political loyalty at least as much as a purely religious centre.

But it is equally possible to argue that Haggai's oracles—and certainly also those of Zechariah 1-8—are essentially concerned with the religious community, and that the order and security brought about by Persian conquests were to be interpreted as the God-given opportunity for the Jewish community in Jerusalem to devote itself with renewed vigour to the worship of its God, without the burden of political involvement which had led to the disasters of the previous century. (Similar arguments have sometimes been put forward with regard to the origins of Christianity: it has been maintained that the widespread diffusion of Christianity was made possible by the peace brought about by universal Roman rule. The apparently favourable attitude to the Romans in Luke-Acts, for example, would provide an instructive comparison with the attitude of Haggai and Zechariah 1-8 to the Persian rulers.)

Certainty in this matter is impossible to achieve, partly because our knowledge of the detailed historical circumstances of the period is fragmentary, but still more because the words of Haggai and Zechariah have come down to us in a particular editorial setting which has interpreted them for its own distinctive purposes. The prophets themselves, that is to say, no longer speak directly to us: we hear them only indirectly through the editorial framework of the present books. It is to the nature and purpose of that framework that we must now turn.

Further Reading

The quantity of secondary literature on prophetism is immense, and no attempt is here made to give a comprehensive listing. Among general treatments that provide a background to the points raised in this chapter the following may be noted:

K. Koch, *The Prophets, Vol. 2*, London: SCM Press, 1983, 159-75.

R. Coggins, A. Phillips & M. Knibb (eds.), *Israel's Prophetic Tradition*, Cambridge: Cambridge University Press, 1982. (Within this survey of problems relating to the prophetic tradition note especially R. Mason, 'The Prophets of the Restoration', 137-54.)

J. Blenkinsopp, *A History of Prophecy in Israel*, London: SPCK, 1984, 225-42. (This chapter is preceded by a very useful bibliography.)

The particular 'court and cult' issue is discussed by:

F.M. Cross, *Canaanite Myth and Hebrew Epic*, London: Oxford University Press, 1973, especially 223-29.

D.L. Petersen, *Late Israelite Prophecy*, Missoula, Montana: Scholars Press, 1977, 1-12.

P.D. Hanson, *The Dawn of Apocalyptic*, Philadelphia: Fortress Press, 1979, 1-31. (See especially the Excursus, 'The History of Prophecy in Israel', 12-16.)

R.P. Carroll, 'Twilight of Prophecy or Dawn of Apocalyptic?', *JSOT* 14 (1979), 3-35. (This is essentially a review article of Hanson's *The Dawn of Apocalyptic*, but has its own important insights relevant to the discussion.)

An interesting study which challenges the received view of prophetism as a long-established activity through much of the people's history is A.G. Auld, 'Prophets through the Looking Glass', *JSOT* 27 (1983), 3-23; see also the responses by R. Carroll and H.G.M. Williamson, and a further note by Auld himself, in the same issue of *JSOT*.

3

THE EDITORIAL
FRAMEWORK OF
HAGGAI AND
ZECHARIAH 1-8

A N IMPORTANT STUDY of the editorial framework of Haggai
and Zechariah 1-8 was carried out some years ago by the
Dutch scholar W.A.M. Beuken, and published in a German
translation in 1967. Frequent reference will be made to this work in
this section. Also relevant is the article by R.A. Mason referred to in
Chapter 2.

What is this 'editorial framework'? It would be generally agreed
that none of the words of the Old Testament prophets has come
down to us directly, without some process of arranging and ordering.
Prophets were essentially speakers, and the very process of setting
down their words in writing implies editorial and redactional
activity. Earlier scholars regarded those who engaged in this process
with some disdain: the real concern of scholarship was to recover
those words which could safely be attributed to the prophet himself;
material which was secondary to the prophet was also of secondary
importance. More recently, however, a good deal of attention has
been paid to this editorial process, often with the conviction that this
editing will not have been simply a neutral matter of conveying the
prophet's words as accurately as possible, but will have been inspired
by particular aims on the part of the editors: a portrait, not a
photograph.

With many of the pre-exilic prophets this editorial process remains
very elusive. Its exact extent, its purpose, the group by whom and the
milieu in which it was carried out—all these remain hotly disputed
questions. (In current discussion argument rages in particular on the
question of the propriety of speaking of a Deuteronomic redaction of
the pre-exilic prophets.) With Haggai and Zechariah, however, the

quest seems to be a little less difficult, since there is at least fairly general agreement about the existence of an editorial framework, and also about its extent. This can most clearly be seen in Zechariah, where the 'night visions' in 1.7–6.15 are preceded and followed by material of a very different kind in 1.1-6 and chs. 7 and 8. Haggai does not at first sight present such a sharp contrast between different types of material, but it is clear that there also a good deal of what constitutes the present form of the book can scarcely have come directly from the prophet himself. Frequently, for example, he is spoken of in the third person, and the effect of his oracles upon his audience is noted.

Hag. 1.12-15 provides a clear example of this type of material. It is an account of the effect of Haggai's preaching upon the leaders of the community, in which the only words attributed to the prophet himself are 'I am with you, says the LORD' (v. 13). It has often been noted (e.g. by Mason, Commentary, 17) that this brief account differs in character from Haggai's own oracles. The latter are primarily addressed to the community as a whole, whereas this account is more concerned with the reaction of the leaders. It may also be noted with reference to this section that the NEB suggests that its 'original order' may be different from that in which it has come down to us. Whatever may be thought of the propriety of such suggested re-ordering, as if there were a hidden Bible lying somewhere behind our present Bible, it may certainly be noted that the likelihood of such changes of order would in itself be a pointer to editorial activity.

Indications of editorial activity are also one reason for the almost universally held modern view, to which reference has already been made, that Zechariah 9–14 are to be sharply differentiated from chs. 1–8 and come from quite a different background. That this differentiation is not simply a fancy attributable to the ingenuity of modern scholars may be illustrated by a consideration of the various introductory formulae that are employed.

In Haggai and Zechariah 1–8 there is regularly used the same introductory formula which relates the words which follow to the year of the reign of Darius, and spells out a specific month and day of the month. This is found in Hag. 1.1, 15 (see Chapter 4 for consideration of the problems relating to the ordering of the material at this point); 2.1, 10, 20; Zech. 1.1, 7; 7.1. Again, a linkage is provided by the use of the formula 'The word of the LORD came'

(Hag. 1.1, 3; 2.2, 10, 20; Zech. 1.1; 7.1, 8; 8.1, 18). Here, however, there is one slight difference, for which no entirely satisfactory explanation has been found. In Haggai the formula following this phrase is normally '*by* Haggai', whereas in Zechariah it is '*to* Zechariah'. We might suppose that in some way the status of the two was perceived to be different; but such a conclusion should be guarded against since in one passage in Haggai (2.20) the same form of words occurs as is otherwise found in Zechariah.

None of these forms is found in the latter part of Zechariah. There, by contrast, we find that the two main sections are introduced by the Hebrew word *massa*, which occurs also at Mal. 1.1. Most modern versions (e.g. the RSV) translate this as 'Oracle', though the word seems to be linked etymologically with the verb meaning 'to lift up', so that the noun would mean something lifted up, that is, a 'burden'; and this is the translation found in older versions (e.g. the RV).

The natural conclusion to be drawn from this brief analysis is that at some stage in the redactional process Haggai and Zechariah 1–8 were linked together, and that similarly Zechariah 9–14 was closely associated with Malachi. With regard to Zechariah 9–14 and Malachi, it must be acknowledged that the similarities do not extend beyond the introductory word into the body of the material that follows, and there is no obvious sign of an identifiable purpose underlying the redactional process, nor any agreement as to the extent and nature of that process. With Haggai and Zechariah 1–8, however, more detailed study has been undertaken and more promising results achieved.

As has already been indicated, the Dutch scholar W.A.M. Beuken played a major part in initiating the modern discussion. His main conclusion was that there are strong links between Haggai and Zechariah in their present form and the work of the Chronicler. (It should be noted that the common view, shared by Beuken, that the Chronicler's work included Ezra–Nehemiah as well as 1 and 2 Chronicles has recently been challenged: see especially H.G.M. Williamson, *Israel in the Books of Chronicles* [Cambridge: Cambridge University Press, 1977] and *1 and 2 Chronicles* [New Century Bible], 1982.) Beuken's conclusion has been disputed, especially by Williamson, who noted (*1 and 2 Chronicles*, 101) that some particular phrases characteristic of the editorial material of Haggai and Zechariah 1–8, such as *Yahweh Sebaoth*, 'the LORD of hosts', do not occur in Chronicles. However, Beuken's view of the Chronicler's work was that it was produced not by a single author but by a group or school: he uses such phrases as 'the Chronistic milieu'. Consequently his general point about a relationship between it and Haggai and Zechariah 1–8 is not necessarily invalidated by Williamson's point about the occurrence of particular phrases, since his theory would allow for some variability of expression.

Beuken argued that there are a number of characteristic features of the editorial framework of Haggai and Zechariah 1–8 which suggest that this 'Chronistic milieu' is its most likely place of origin. In addition to the dating scheme already mentioned, which corresponds closely with that found in Ezra, he noted that the relation between prophet and king in Haggai 1 compares closely with that found in the books of Chronicles, and that the pattern of sin / affliction / repentance / grace, which characterizes Haggai 1, is also a regular device of the Chronicler (e.g. 2 Chron. 12.1-8). More controversial is his suggestion concerning Hag. 2.10-14, where he argued that Haggai's original condemnations of the Jerusalem community have been given an anti-Samaritan slant by the Chronicler. For this to be persuasive it would be necessary to establish that the work of the Chronicler contained an anti-Samaritan polemic, and it has been widely argued that such terms are in fact anachronistic, since the decisive breach between the Samaritans and the Jews of Jerusalem came later than any plausible date for the Chronicler. (See Coggins, *Samaritans and Jews*, Oxford: Blackwell, 1975, especially 68-72.)

Beuken reached similar conclusions with regard to Zechariah 1–8 with significant modifications because of the different arrangement of the material: the series of visions in 1.7–6.15 has not been interpolated with detailed editorial comment or redaction; rather, the evidence of the editorial hand is to be seen in the opening verses (1.1- 6) and in chs. 7 and 8. 1.1–6 are likened by Beuken, in both form and content, to the Levitical sermons found in Chronicles; the particular detailed comparison he offers is with 2 Chron. 30.6-9. (He provides a point-by-point tabular analysis on p. 91.) (The 'Levitical sermon' in Chronicles was a form first identified by G. von Rad: see his 'The Levitical Sermon in the Books of Chronicles', in *The Problem of the Hexateuch and other Essays*, Edinburgh and London: Oliver & Boyd, 1966, re-issued London: SCM Press, 1984, 270-80.) A further Levitical sermon may be traceable in Zech. 7.7-14 (v. 8 is a gloss interrupting the flow of the original material), and yet another in 8.9-17.

Beuken's conclusion, applied specifically to Zechariah 7–8 but equally relevant to the whole editorial process, is that the final compilers, who are to be located within the Chronistic milieu, were using the Haggai and Zechariah traditions as the basis for an appeal to the community of their own day, perhaps a century later, to take the lessons of the past to heart, and to see how God had raised up prophets at times of crisis to encourage his people and to keep them on the right path.

The other scholar who has made a particular study of the editorial framework of these books is R.A. Mason. In addition to the article already mentioned, he makes reference to this issue in his commentary, and in an article discussing a number of aspects of the recent study of these prophets, 'The Prophets of the Restoration' (Coggins, Phillips and Knibb, *Israel's Prophetic Tradition*, 137-54). There is a substantial measure of agreement between Mason and Beuken, but Mason is not convinced that the analogies pointed out by Beuken necessarily lead to the conclusion that the editorial process took place in the Chronistic milieu. He talks in more general terms of 'theocratic circles', and in this he shows the influence of the discussion which we shall need to consider more fully in Chapter 6. Without anticipating that fuller consideration we may simply note here that the view implied by Mason is one that sees in the Israel of this period two main 'parties'. One of these embodied the outlook found in the latter part of the book of Isaiah (and possibly, though this is much more disputed, also in Zechariah 9–14). Its world-view was visionary and eschatological: it looked forward to God's dramatic and decisive intervention in the affairs of his people. The other is sometimes described as 'theocratic'. It was convinced of the reality of God's rule in the present; it took a quietist line in political matters, and broadly represented the viewpoint of the ruling groups in Jerusalem during the Second Temple period. On the view here being discussed, Haggai will have been an early representative of such a point of view, and the editorial milieu in which his oracles reached their final form will also have been associated with the same theocratic understanding of Israel's position.

There are problems associated with such a reconstruction (see Chapter 6), but it is certainly true that the dominant concern of Haggai, and to a lesser extent of Zechariah, was with the temple. It is therefore probable that it was in 'temple circles' that their oracles were brought into their final form. At this point it may be important to remind ourselves that the temple was not simply the ancient equivalent of a modern church building. There were two other aspects of temples in the ancient world. First, they were regarded as the 'house' of the god in whose honour they were built in a much more direct sense than the way in which modern church buildings can be spoken of as the 'house of God'. It is important to keep this point in mind when we read such a phrase as 'my house that lies in ruins' (Hag. 1.9): there were those in ancient Israel (and both Haggai and those who edited his oracles were among their number) who regarded the temple as essential to the community's religious life, since it was there that their God dwelt.

Secondly, we should remember the political importance of temples. The temple of Solomon has sometimes been described as a 'royal chapel', and, although this is an inadequate description, it nevertheless serves to emphasize the political importance of the community's chief religious building. The temple about which Haggai and Zechariah were concerned was to be built under imperial patronage: it would thus serve as a clear reminder that the community which joined in worship there accepted its status within the Persian empire.

If what has been said about the context in which Haggai and Zechariah 1–8 were edited has any force, this will have further important implications for our understanding of these two prophetic collections and the individual figures from whom they are named. Haggai and Zechariah are referred to together in the book of Ezra (5.1; 6.14), and it is in fact from the historical context supplied by that book that we normally reconstruct their historical setting. That is to say, the early chapters of Ezra picture an 'end' to the exile, the return of the faithful Jewish community to Jerusalem from their temporary sojourn in Babylon, and their commitment to the re-establishment of their religious life, spurred on by the two prophets. Were we simply to read the two prophetic collections by themselves, this is not quite the impression that we should gain. Haggai in particular makes no reference to exile or return, and neither prophet seems to be in any way aware that a turning-point in the community's life—the end of the exile—has been reached.

Many scholars have raised questions about the historical reliability of the reconstruction in Ezra (see also above, Chapter 1), and it is necessary to ask whether it is in fact to be understood as a historical account, or rather as a theological appraisal of the importance of

exile as an experience through which the genuine community must
necessarily have passed. Perhaps, as we have already noted (above,
p. 10), it is misleading to speak of an 'end' of the exile.

If this is a correct interpretation of the purpose of Ezra, it may help
to shed more light on the nature of the editorial process which has
been applied to the words of Haggai and Zechariah. It remains likely
that that process took place in circles akin to those which produced
Chronicles and Ezra-Nehemiah. It is easy to envisage that in such
circles the particular way in which the role of those prophets was
understood was to see them as having been responsible, as God's
instruments, for encouraging the community to make a new start.
This would readily account for the prominence and approval with
which they are described in Ezra 5—and in this connection it is
important to remember that such specific reference in the 'historical
books' to the activity of the prophets after whom books are named is
very exceptional.

By such editorial work the words of the prophets themselves were
given fresh authentication and set within a specific context as the
restorers of Israel at the beginning of a new period of divine favour.
Beuken and Mason both rightly stress the importance in the editorial
framework (e.g. Hag. 1.13) of the theme of the presence of God with
his people as a particular mark of that favour. It is in some such way
as this, following the example of these first editors, that most later
interpreters have understood Haggai and Zechariah; it now remains
to consider to what extent it is possible to penetrate behind this
editorial framework to discover how far the original message of the
prophets themselves is recoverable, and, if it *is* recoverable, how far it
corresponds to the perception of the editors. It may perhaps be added
as a postscript to this section that the desire to unearth the original,
historical nucleus is in no way intended to devalue the increasingly
common stress on looking at the final form of the text. That is a
perfectly legitimate exercise; but it must not be allowed to crowd out
the search for historical origins which has played a major part in Old
Testament study for the last two centuries.

Further Reading

As already indicated, there are two main studies in which the subject matter of this chapter is discussed:

W.A.M. Beuken, *Haggai-Sacharja 1–8. Studien zur Überlieferungs-geschichte der frühnachexilischen Prophetie*, Assen, 1967.

R.A. Mason, 'The Purpose of the "Editorial Framework" of the Book of Haggai', *VT* 27 (1977), 413-21.

Mason adds further brief comments in his essay,

'The Prophets of the Restoration', in Coggins, Phillips and Knibb, *Israel's Prophetic Tradition*, Cambridge, 1982, especially 144-46.

The matter is, of course, discussed in all the major commentaries. But whereas older commentaries were often somewhat dismissive of the role of editors, more recent writings devote a good deal of attention to this matter. See for example:

D.L. Petersen, *Haggai and Zechariah 1–8* (OTL), London, 1984, 32-39 (on Haggai), 120-25 (on Zechariah).

The article 'Zechariah, Book of' in *IDB(S)*, Abingdon, 1975, by P.D. Hanson discusses the structure of Zechariah 1-8 from the point of view of its socio-religious setting, as distinct from the literary concerns which have here been considered. The nature of the editorial process has also come to play a more prominent part in recent Introductions to the Old Testament. See especially:

B.S. Childs, *Introduction to the Old Testament as Scripture*, London, 1979, 467-70, 476-79.

4

HAGGAI

IT HAS OFTEN been maintained that one of the indications of a decline in the significance of prophetism is that the later prophets concentrated on only one theme, or a very small number of themes. Thus, for example, Haggai is compared unfavourably with the great prophets of the eighth century, whose message had been addressed to many aspects of the nation's life. Even when this limitation is not equated with a decline in power, it is still regarded as almost axiomatic. Mason, for example, in his contribution to *Israel's Prophetic Tradition*, can assert that 'the oracles (of Haggai) reflect a simple consistent message' (p. 142). This message is that the hardships then being suffered by the community are 'judgements from God for their failure to rebuild the temple'.

This, however, is one of those themes which can appear very differently according to the context in which they are placed. Mason's judgment here has not always been accepted; and indeed, as we shall see below, Mason himself expresses it in slightly different terms later in his article, when he stresses the eschatological dimension in Haggai's preaching. His view that Haggai in his oracles was 'directly addressing the community of returned exiles' would also not be universally accepted. As we have already noted, it is an inference drawn from the editorial framework rather than the contents of Haggai's own oracles which leads to the supposition that their addressees were returned exiles. For Haggai himself they were the Jerusalem community, who were neglecting what should be a basic identifying mark of any religious community: the temple as the centre of their worship and as the place which was the focus of their identity as the Yahweh-community. (The sociological implications of the notion of the temple as providing such a focus are interestingly explored by D.L. Petersen in his Commentary: see especially pp. 30f.)

In Haggai's time the generation that had known of a living temple in which God's glory was manifested had now effectively passed away (2.3), and they found it perfectly possible to survive without a temple (or at least, without a properly restored temple: as we have already noted in Chapter 1, there is no certainty whether the site was ruinous, or whether some restoration had already taken place but on a scale now regarded by Haggai as inadequate). This attitude seemed to Haggai to reflect a perverted sense of priorities. Now a more ambitious work of rebuilding could be embarked upon; that such a plan was possible seems to have been common ground between Haggai and his hearers (1.2).

We saw in the last section that it is probably only the editorial framework which places Haggai in an 'end-of-exile' context, and we should not therefore assume that for Haggai himself, or for his hearers, return from exile and rebuilding of the temple were inextricably bound together. It may well be that Haggai himself simply had the latter point as his primary concern.

But then the question arises: was this concern for the rebuilding of the temple in fact Haggai's *only* concern? It has sometimes been implied that he supposed that all other blessings would automatically follow upon proper attention to the temple. Just as current troubles were due to its neglect (2.15-17), so future blessing could be guaranteed if rebuilding was taken seriously in hand (2.18f.).

It would be hard to deny that there *is* a link here of a kind which would have been inconceivable to some of the pre-exilic prophets (cf. Jeremiah's scornful attack on those who put all their trust in 'the temple of the LORD' [Jer. 7.4]; yet it is also true that for Haggai this is not the whole story. Ackroyd has rightly pointed out (*Exile and Restoration*, 156f.) that 'the failure to rebuild is much more than a matter of reconstruction of a building. It is the reordering of a Temple so that it is a fit place for worship. Rebuilding is therefore linked to the condition of the people for the service of God'.

This gives us an indication that there is another important element in the message of Haggai. Although, as we have just seen, there is nothing in his oracles which demands as their context the return from Babylonian exile, it is undeniable that they recognize the existence of a new situation in the life of the community. Thus with 2.1-9: its immediate concern is with the rebuilding of the temple, but it is also apparent that a larger context is envisaged. God is assuring the people of his lasting presence with them, a presence which is recalled in the past history of his dealings with them ('the promise that I made you when you came out of Egypt'), which is assured as present reality ('My spirit abides among you; fear not'), and which is promised as a sign of future glory ('I will shake all nations, so that the treasures of all nations shall come in'). We shall need to recall the breadth of the theological scope of statements of this kind when we consider the argument that has been put forward, that Haggai is limited to a purely establishment-centred, theocratic viewpoint (Chapter 6 below).

A restored community would need effective leaders, both political and religious; and this supplies the context for the concern shown by Haggai for Zerubbabel and Joshua. With one exception these are addressed or spoken of together throughout the book—a clear indication of the close relation between political and religious leadership which Haggai envisages. There is no suggestion that Haggai simply had in mind a return to pre-exilic days with the Davidic monarchy in control of an independent nation-state. A dual leadership of the community's efforts was needed.

In one passage, however, there is an exception to the customary combined reference. This is the concluding oracle 2.20-23, which, together with a closely comparable passage in Zechariah 4, suggests that 'messianic' expectations were associated with Zerubbabel. Part of the difficulty in interpreting this passage lies in the fact that it seems that its intention may, partly at least, have been to function as a corrective to an earlier prophetic passage, Jer. 22.24. There Coniah (i.e. Jehoiachin), who was the king of Judah in 597, had been described as a 'signet-ring' (*hotham*) on Yahweh's own hand, whose fate was to be torn off and given to his enemies. Part of Haggai's purpose here is to give assurance that this rejection of the Davidic line is not permanent. A later member of the same dynasty could be acceptable to God, and so Zerubbabel himself could be described as a *hotham*.

There is no means of knowing in what specific way Haggai's hopes were centred upon Zerubbabel. (The background to this oracle is discussed in detail by K.M. Beyse, *Serubbabel und die Königser-wartungen der Propheten Haggai und Sacharja* (Stuttgart, 1972), 50-66, who sees in this passage a re-interpretation of the Jeremiah text in the light of the kind of hopes for the Davidic line which are expressed in 2 Samuel 7. It is a word of encouragement for the community, which is invited to envisage the restoration of Davidic rule with

Zerubbabel as Yahweh's vicegerent.) We should note that there is no direct suggestion that Zerubbabel will have 'royal' or 'messianic' status of a precisely defined kind: the people were under the rule of a Persian king. But it is clear that Haggai intended to reassure the community that the age of Yahweh's power to act was by no means over.

There are some other points of detail to which attention should also be drawn for a proper understanding of Haggai. We should note that while the oracles of earlier prophets had for the most part been expressed in poetry, Haggai, if the RSV is to be followed, shares with Malachi the unique distinction of being wholly composed in prose. (Students of Hebrew will, however, note a difference here between the older and the more recent editions of the main critical edition, the *Biblia Hebraica* of R. Kittel. In the older edition Haggai is printed in prose throughout, whereas in the more recent [BHS] edition 1.4-11, 2.3-9 and certain other fragments are printed as poetry. There is in fact some disagreement between commentators on the question whether it is more appropriate to speak of Haggai's oracles as true poetry or as rhythmic prose. It is probably impossible to make a sharp distinction between these two modes of speech.)

Of greater moment is the one major difficulty which arises with regard to the structure of the book, which is for the most part clear and unproblematic. The exception is 1.15. It is almost universally agreed that the last phrase of this verse ('in the second year of Darius the king') serves as an introduction to the following section, and it is so printed in most translations. But this leaves 1.15a without any relation to the surrounding context. RSV makes the best of a bad job by treating it as the end of the preceding section, but this goes against the regular usage found elsewhere in the book. NEB, in a footnote, suggests that the material has become disordered, and proposes a very complex re-ordering. More straightforwardly, many commentators (e.g. among recent writers Mason and Amsler) have proposed that 1.15a should be affixed to 2.15-19, which has only a very tenuous connection with 2.10-14 and has no separate introduction.

This in turn draws attention to the fact that 2.10-14 is a passage which stands very much by itself, whose theme is not closely related to the remainder of the book. Two points of particular interest deserve to be noted here. First, the passage provides a unique example in the prophetic collections in the Old Testament of what was apparently a regular priestly form. In cases of uncertainty concerning cultic matters, it was necessary to ask the priests for a verdict upon ritual purity and impurity. (The New Testament shows that such a custom was still recognized in the Judaism of that period, when Jesus bids the man cleansed of a skin disease to obtain a priestly verdict concerning his ritual condition [Mark 1.44].) Such a verdict was a priestly *torah*; the word means 'guidance' or 'decision' (it was only later that it came to be applied to the whole body of the Pentateuch).

This use of the *torah* form is interesting in itself, and might lend support to the view that Haggai was a cultic prophet closely associated with the priests of the Jerusalem sanctuary, though we should beware of supposing that prophets could never use forms of speech which originated from milieux different from their own. But the point at issue is how to understand the application of the principle spelt out here to the group described as 'this people' (2.14). There has been much discussion as to the identity of 'this people'.

The natural assumption would be that the reference is to the Jerusalem community, which is referred to in 1.2 in the same words. But a difficulty arises from the fact that 'this people' is here being implicitly condemned. Chapter 1 describes how the community has begun work on the restoration of the temple, as Haggai had urged; but now, three months later (if the date in 2.10 is taken at its face value), it appears to be said that their work is 'unclean' despite this obedience to Haggai's preaching. Accordingly, some commentators have supposed that 'this people' in 2.14 must have a different referent. In particular, as Petersen puts it (Commentary, 80) 'one answer has dominated the critical literature': that 'this people' are a group *set over against* the faithful Jerusalem community, most probably one centred in the territory of the former Northern kingdom, around Samaria. If this were so, we should have one of the earliest pieces of evidence for the emergence of the Samaritans.

This view, though still widely held, has been criticized recently on various grounds. There is in fact no basis in the book of Haggai itself for seeing here a reference to Samaria; and it is now widely held that the origins of Samaritanism should be sought at a much later period (see Coggins, *Samaritans and Jews*, especially 50-52). Moreover, the content of the passage makes it clear that it is not the people as such, but the 'work of their hands' and 'what they offer' (v. 14) which is unclean. It seems more satisfactory, therefore, to see the warning to 'this people' as addressed to the Jerusalem community itself, as in

1.2. Even so holy a 'work of their hands' as the restoration of the Jerusalem temple was not in itself a guarantee of sanctification. From this there follow two concluding points which need to be made with regard to Haggai. First, the book shows us that his concerns were indeed wider than the restoration of the temple; we are also offered links back to the pre-exilic prophets, with their frequent warnings against false trust in human efforts. Although the words of Haggai (or at least those of them which have been set down in writing and preserved for us) are on a small scale, they embody the characteristic concerns of the great prophetic tradition. Secondly, this larger perspective raises a further question: was Haggai concerned only with the immediate standing of the community before God, or should we see his concerns as on an altogether larger scale? Mason, for example, concludes his discussion of different interpretations of Hag. 2.10-14 with the claim that 'Again, we see the centrality of eschatological hope to the preaching of Haggai. He has no other message' (*Israel's Prophetic Tradition*, 144). Such an eschatological claim on Haggai's behalf is sharply at odds with the viewpoint of Hanson and others that Haggai represented a theocratic position opposed to the eschatological standpoint of the proto-apocalyptists of his day. This is an issue to which we shall need to return in Chapter 6.

Further Reading

The issues discussed in this chapter are, of course, discussed in all commentaries on Haggai; and this is perhaps the appropriate point at which to make reference to the available commentaries. All of those listed contain bibliographies, including references to commentaries in languages other than English, and to articles on specific points.

> J.G. Baldwin, *Haggai, Zechariah, Malachi* (TOTC) London, 1972 (a clear exposition of a conservative viewpoint. There is no separate bibliographical section, but there are many references in the footnotes to other works).
>
> D.R. Jones, *Haggai, Zechariah and Malachi* (TC), London, 1962 (the particular interest of this work lies in its unusual views on Zech. 9–14; on Haggai it is a brief straightforward commentary).
>
> R.A. Mason, *The Books of Haggai, Zechariah and Malachi* (CBC), Cambridge, 1977 (this is very brief, but it is in effect a distillation of the author's other studies of Haggai, to

which reference has already been made).

H.G. Mitchell, in Mitchell, J.M.P. Smith, and J.A. Bewer, *Haggai, Zechariah, Malachi and Jonah* (ICC), Edinburgh, 1912 (this is now inevitably dated, but is an immensely detailed study which is still valuable for reference, particularly on philological points).

D.L. Petersen, *Haggai and Zechariah 1–8* (OTL), London 1984 (the most recent and perhaps most generally useful commentary currently available).

R.L. Smith, *Micah–Malachi* (WBC) Waco, 1984 (pp. 145-63 of this general commentary on the later Minor Prophets deal with Haggai; bibliographies, textual notes and form-critical comments are included as well as the commentary proper).

D.W. Thomas, 'The Book of Haggai', in *IB*, IV, New York, 1956 (although in a general series, this brief commentary by a distinguished philologist retains its value).

Reference should also be made here to P.R. Ackroyd, *Exile and Restoration*, London, 1968, chs. 9 & 10. This is not in commentary form, but it deals with the issues discussed in this chapter and in the commentaries.

5
ZECHARIAH 1—8

ZECHARIAH IS regularly associated with Haggai. This linkage can be traced as far back as the book of Ezra, in which the two prophets are twice (5.1; 6.14) spoken of without differentiation as those whose ministry was decisive in bringing about the rebuilding of the Jerusalem temple. This custom of grouping the two prophets together has also characterized modern scholarly treatments, and we saw in Chapter 3 that there is some justification for this in the way in which the same editorial framework has been provided for both of them.

No very detailed study of the text of Zechariah 1-8 is, however, required to see that, apart from the editorial framework (1.1-6; 7.1-8.23), the contents of these chapters differ very strikingly from what is found in Haggai. Haggai remained in the tradition of the prophet as *speaker*, passing on to individuals or to the community words which, he was convinced, constituted a message from God. But there was another tradition related to the prophetic role: that of the prophet as *see-er*, the one who became privy to the secrets of the divine plan through visionary experience. It was in this tradition that Zechariah stood.

The rendering 'see-er' is not a spelling or printing mistake. In English we tend to assume that 'speaking' and 'seeing' relate to quite different modes of experience; but in fact there are many passages in the Old Testament where 'seer' and 'prophet' seem to be used interchangeably, and it would certainly not be possible from this usage to differentiate between them on the grounds either of their experience or of the form of their message. the best-known passage of this kind is 1 Sam. 9.9, which ends with the note, 'for he who is now called a prophet was formerly called a seer'. (For discussion of this, and of various modern theories that particular definable religious types can be discerned behind the present description of 'prophets' and 'seers', see J.R. Porter, 'The Origins of Prophecy in Israel', in Coggins, Phillips and Knibb [eds.], *Israel's Prophetic Tradition*, especially 13-25.)

Precise reasons for using sometimes the word *nabî* (prophet), sometimes the words *roeh* or *hozeh* (both normally translated seer) cannot now be established. What is beyond serious dispute is that the importance of visionary experience was established in Israel's prophetic tradition long before the time of Zechariah. It is inherent in the title of several of the prophetic books. The book of Isaiah, for example, begins, 'The vision of Isaiah. . . which he saw'; and there is no doubt that the contents of this 'vision' cannot be confined to the famous vision described in Isaiah 6. Isaiah 6 has often, whether rightly or wrongly, been regarded as an inaugural vision experienced at the very outset of Isaiah's ministry, and so might be regarded as a special case. But it is clear that as far back as Amos, c. 750, specific visionary experiences played an important part in prophetic experience. In Amos 7 and 8 each item in a series of visions begins with the expression (in slightly varying forms), 'Thus the LORD God showed me; behold . . . '. (The verb translated 'showed' could be translated, more literally, though also more clumsily, 'caused me to see'.) This visionary tradition is also found in Jeremiah (e.g. 4.23-26 and the visions attached to the account of his call in ch. 1).

It is, however, with Ezekiel that these visionary features become particularly prominent, and it has therefore been usual to see here the closest links with Zechariah. (We shall consider in the next chapter whether such formal similarities extend also to a similarity of role between the two prophets, so that each might be regarded as representative of a 'theocratic' as against an 'eschatological' prophetic understanding of God's dealings with his people.) It is perhaps inherent in the very nature of visions and visionary experience that interpretation will be needed: what is seen might convey very different messages to different people. Certainly with Ezekiel it is beyond dispute that greater complexity has arisen, so that elaborate and detailed explanations become necessary. Again, whereas in earlier prophets some at least of the things seen in visions were objects of everyday experience (e.g. the basket of summer fruit, Amos 8.1f.), in Ezekiel this simple directness (never the whole of the story even in Amos, as we are warned by the visions of the divine in 7.4 and 9.1) has given place to a much more complex, not to say contrived, visionary experience.

In the book of Zechariah in its present form we find a series of eight visions. There has been much discussion whether this eightfold series is original, or whether the vision in ch. 3 should be regarded as a later addition to an earlier series consisting of seven visions. The main reasons for the latter view are to be found in the formal differences in its presentation: the characteristic introductory phrase ('I lifted up my eyes and saw') is absent; the interpreting angel plays no part; there is no mysterious object seen which needs explanation. Indeed, this vision resembles in many ways those passages in earlier prophets in which the prophet is admitted to the divine council and sees or hears the decisions which God is in process of reaching, along with his attendants, about matters on earth. The words of Micaiah in 1 Kgs 22.19-23 are a classic example of this form, which G.B. Caird has likened to the idea of a modern press gallery in a council chamber (*The Language and Imagery of the Bible*, London: Duckworth, 1980, 178).

These formal differences in ch. 3 from the other visions have not only led to the widely held view that this vision is a later insertion into an original set of seven; they have also occasioned the suggestion that in the process of insertion some re-arrangement of the existing order of the material took place. This is reflected, for example, by the NEB translation, in which 4.1-3, 11-14 are placed before ch. 3 with 4.4-10 following it. There is no doubt that 4.11 refers back to 4.3, and the immediate juxtaposition of these verses in NEB makes this clearer; whether as a general principle a modern translation is justified in trying to re-create some more perfect Bible behind our present Bible is much more questionable. (See Mason's commentary, which is specifically on the NEB, 45f., for a discussion of this particular re-arrangement.)

To revert to the visions as a whole. While on grounds of form there is a strong case for seeing ch. 3 as a later addition, with regard to content there is a strong similarity between the whole series of visions. Even among the seven normally taken as primary, the form is not identical. There is a brief introduction, but the wording is not stereotyped: the expression 'I lifted up my eyes and saw' occurs four times (1.18; 2.1; 5.1; 6.1), while the other introductions differ. Each vision is then described in first-person singular form as having been experienced by the prophet himself. It is taken for granted that its meaning is not self-explanatory, and so the prophet seeks an explanation ('What are these?' [1.9, 4.12; 6.4] and similar questions), which is then given to him by an interpreting 'angel' or divine messenger. The first vision is described as having taken place at night (1.8), and so the assumption is commonly made that this is intended to be true of the whole series. However this may be, we should perhaps see in this statement an important link between prophecy and the later apocalypses, in which 'night visions' are a characteristic mode of divine self revelation (cf. Dan. 7.1). This is one of the reasons given by R. North for entitling an article 'Prophecy to Apocalyptic via Zechariah': 'First-Zechariah's dream-riddles resemble canonical Daniel, the normative example of apocalyptic' (70).

North's description of this material as 'dream-riddles' immediately raises the question of the interpretation of these visions. The first issue that needs to be considered is the relation of form to content. In other words: are the visions simply an elaborate means of conveying a message that might equally have been conveyed by means of prophetic oracles, or does the visionary form imply some radically different kind of message? Put in an extreme way (as is rarely done explicitly, but often by implication), the former alternative would make of the visions little more than visual aids, a dramatic means of getting the message over to the audience. This is clearly unsatisfactory: the visions are set out as the consequence of a type of prophetic experience which is significant for its own sake. The reference to visions being experienced at night raises the question whether modern study of the psychology of dreams can help in the interpretation of the visions of Zechariah and other prophets and apocalyptists; opinions on this matter remain sharply divided. (See the discussion in D.L. Petersen, *Haggai & Zechariah 1–8*, 111-20, and the various studies cited in the footnotes.)

The visions, then, represent a distinctive mode of experience, but it may still be that it is their interpretation which is of the most crucial significance in the understanding of Zechariah. (This is probably the majority opinion among scholars: see for example Beuken's study, 237-58, where he analyses two distinct types of vision here, yet concludes that it is God's message to his people which is the crucial element for their understanding.) If we first consider this matter of interpretation, it will soon be apparent that there are similarities with, but also important differences from, Haggai. Both Haggai and Zechariah had as primary concerns the way in which God would bring about his saving act on behalf of the community. It is interesting in this respect that, for example, Ackroyd, in his discussion of the two prophets, found it practicable to arrange the message of each of them around the same three themes: the temple; the new community and the new age; and the people's response (*Exile and Restoration*, chs. 10 and 11).

But there are also important respects in which the two prophets differ. First, Zechariah was clearly one of the former exiles who had returned from Babylon, whereas we have no such information about Haggai. The reasons for making this assertion about Zechariah are, first, the description of him as 'son of Berechiah, son of Iddo, the prophet' (1.2), which has often been taken to indicate a connection with the references in Neh. 12.4, 16 to a Zechariah of the house of Iddo with Babylonian links. This point should perhaps not be pressed, for it seems that the genealogical link may be a redactional addition intended to establish a link between our Zechariah and the 'Zechariah the son of Jeberechiah' referred to in Isa. 8.2. Secondly, however—and this is more convincing—there are a number of Babylonian allusions in the visions themselves. (These are discussed by Amsler, in his commentary on Zechariah, 49.) 2.6ff. gain their point from the notion of a return from Babylon to Jerusalem: the 'foe from the north' referred to in earlier prophetic oracles has no continuing power over the people of Yahweh. Babylon is referred to specifically in 5.11, and is possibly alluded to elsewhere. More generally, it is often maintained that the imagery of the visions betrays a Mesopotamian background. This last point, however, should be treated with caution, since it is not easy to be confident in deciding how far such imagery arises from the visionary's actual life-experience, and how far it is dependent on the particular literary traditions which he had inherited. Nevertheless it seems clear that whereas Haggai was addressing his oracles to the Jerusalem community with little concern for their previous experience, whether or not he had himself been in exile, for Zechariah the idea of return was an important one. It was a first sign of the Lord's saving power at work among his people, and an earnest of further acts of salvation to come.

Another difference between Haggai and Zechariah is to be found in the recipients of their messages. In Haggai, as we have seen (cf. Chapter 4 above), the role of Zerubbabel was strongly emphasized. In Zechariah, by contrast, it is Joshua the high priest who is the particular subject of the message. Zerubbabel is mentioned only in

4.6-10, as the one responsible for the organization of the temple-building; elsewhere it is Joshua who is the object of concern. This in turn raises two further questions about which there has been much dispute: the interpretation of ch. 3, which is addressed solely to Joshua; and the original reference of 6.9-15, which appears as an appendix to the series of visions.

We have already noted that there is some dispute whether ch. 3 should be regarded as an integral part of the series of visions, and this difference extends also to its interpretation. Whereas elsewhere the role of the angel is to supply an interpretation of what the prophet has seen in response to his questions, here the angel is part of the vision. Again, the other visions describe what is seen in terms that are clearly symbolic: horses, horns, lampstands and the like. Here, by contrast, what is seen is the familiar figure of Joshua the high priest, and the vision is simply a device for indicating that he is the recipient of the divine favour.

This point is, in broad outline, clearly enough established by the general tenor of the vision, but there are a number of detailed points which bring it out more specifically. First, the confrontation with 'Satan' (vv. 1f.). In their comments on this section, scholars have been at pains to point out that this figure should not be confused with the Devil, the embodiment of evil seen as a personal figure, such as is found in the New Testament and other later literature: the Hebrew here is '*the* Satan', that is, a member of the heavenly court. Rightly so. But it is also important to bear in mind that the figure as presented here is a hostile one, only too ready to accuse those whom God himself favours. As far as translation is concerned, perhaps 'the Adversary' (as in NEB) is the best solution. Joshua, then, is sure of the Lord's favour over against the Adversary.

Secondly, the promise 'I will clothe you with rich apparel' (v. 4) needs to be understood in the light of the detailed concern for the high-priestly raiment set out in Exodus 28. There was a sense in which the clothes made the man. (Amsler, Commentary, 81, in making this point, draws attention to the Parable of the Prodigal Son [Luke 15.22], where the first sign of the father's welcome is the way in which he clothes his son with the appropriate garments.) Thirdly, and more contentiously, it is sometimes argued that the 'turban' with which Joshua is crowned (v. 5) is essentially a royal garment, and that it is therefore proper to see here the beginnings of that process by which the high priest came to be the ruler of the Jerusalem community, with royal as well as religious symbolism associated with him. (Sirach 50.1-21 is the clearest example of this in the biblical tradition, though the presentation of the high-priestly role in the Passion narratives in the Gospels also gives some indication of the special status accorded to the high priest in the Judaism of that period.)

The fourth point which needs to be borne in mind with regard to Zechariah 3 is in some respects a development of this issue of status. In v. 8 Joshua is described as 'my servant the Branch'. This description is noteworthy in that it brings together two very significant ways of referring to those specially commissioned for a particular role in God's service. Furthermore, these are applied, not, as might have been expected from the usage in Haggai, to the Davidic ruler Zerubbabel, but to the priestly leader of the community. Something more will need to be said on this point in our consideration of Zechariah 6.

With regard to the titles themselves, 'servant' and 'branch', we may note first that the Hebrew word *ṣemaḥ*, 'branch', is used several times in the prophetic literature in contexts which imply the establishment of a particular figure who will fulfil Yahweh's will (Isa. 4.2; Jer. 23.5 [33.15]). This usage is sometimes described as 'messianic', though that can be a misleading term in view of the very different ways in which the terms messiah/messianic are employed by modern scholars. (See J.G. Baldwin, '*ṣemaḥ* as a technical term in the Prophets', *VT* 14 [1964] 93-97.) The remarkable feature of Zech. 3.8, however, is that here *ṣemaḥ* is combined with the other title 'servant', a designation most familiar from the servant passages in Isaiah 40-55, but also a regular way of speaking of the one who is especially favoured by Yahweh. This usage is not confined to the prophets: see for example its application to David in Ps. 89.3, 20. (See the volume on *The Second Isaiah* in this series, by R.N. Whybray [1983], for a discussion of the 'servant' material in Isaiah 40-55.)

The use of the term *ṣemaḥ* is not confined in Zechariah to 3.8. It is found also in 6.12, in a passage which appears to have been appended to the series of night visions, and which has caused very widespread discussion. It is widely held that this is a passage which underwent expansion and development before it reached its present form in the Hebrew Bible, but there is no agreement as to the precise nature of such a development. Two particular points have been the focus of discussion. First, in 6.11 and 14 it appears as though more than one

crown is envisaged, and RSV has 'crown' in each place, with a
marginal note indicating that in the Hebrew text the word is plural,
'crowns'. Some scholars have argued that the word is not a true
plural, but an archaizing form of the singular (so E. Lipiński,
'Recherches sur le livre de Zacharie', *VT* 20 [1970], 34f.); but the
difficulty is that there is no obvious reason why such an archaizing
form should have been used just at this point. Most commentators
have therefore either emended the text to read the singular (so for
example Amsler), or assumed that the plural is correct and that
originally both Joshua and Zerubbabel were to be crowned.

This leads to a second, and related, question. It has been widely
argued that the original reference in these verses was to Zerubbabel,
who was either the only one crowned, or who was crowned alongside
Joshua. It is then suggested that the name of Zerubbabel was omitted
and that of Joshua substituted for it, either because Zerubbabel fell
from favour and was removed from his office by the Persian
authorities, or because of an increasing belief among the Jewish
community that the priestly office was the all-important one (see also
p. 14 above). This, together with other passages relating to Zerubbabel,
has been discussed by R.P. Carroll, as illustrating the problem of
prophecy which failed: Zerubbabel did not fulfil the expectations
associated with him. Carroll suggests that the psychological theory
known as 'cognitive dissonance' may help our understanding of the
way in which the community came to terms with disappointed
expectations (*When Prophecy Failed*, London: SCM Press, 1979,
156-68; this discussion is worthy of attention whether or not it is
accepted that the name of Zerubbabel originally occurred in the
present passage).

That it is not easy to envisage the process by which the
hypothetical change from a reference to Zerubbabel to one to Joshua
in 6.9ff. took place has been shown by Ackroyd (*Exile and
Restoration*, 195-99). Not all will be convinced by his own proposed
solution of the problem, that 'the stress here is laid upon the relation
between the priest(s) and the coming Branch' (197). An alternative
view which has been put forward by Mason is perhaps more
probable: that these verses have been subjected to a redaction which
has changed their emphasis from the literal to the metaphorical sense
of 'building' the temple, and a future, messianic figure is now
envisaged ('The Prophets of the Restoration', 148). There is clearly
no agreement as yet concerning the interpretation of this passage,

nor of its relation to the visions which precede it.

These difficulties with regard to individual passages are matched by a number of serious problems with regard to the meaning of the visions. In the later apocalyptic writings there is often a sense that the meaning of the message is to be hidden from all except the favoured group within the community (cf. the interjection in Mark 13.14, 'Let the reader understand'), and such a sense is already beginning to emerge in Zechariah 1–8. The frequent references to the interpreting angel heighten this impression: the meaning of God's word is no longer self-evident, and an interpretation is necessary. Again, some of the visions themselves are so bizarre that even their surface meaning is far from apparent. This is true of the two visions in ch. 5 of the flying scroll and the woman sitting in the ephah, though it is clear that each is concerned with various social evils still prevalent in the land (cf. in particular vv. 3 and 6). In one sense this reference to social evils shows that Zechariah remained firmly within the prophetic tradition: the eighth-century prophets had been concerned with similar wrongs. Yet the way in which these evils are described and denounced by Zechariah puts a considerable distance between him and his predecessors. We are again reminded of the title of North's article: 'Prophecy to Apocalyptic via Zechariah'. North himself suggests (71) that part of the difference between Zechariah's visions and earlier prophetic oracles may lie in the fact that the earlier prophets had *spoken* their words of warning, whereas Zechariah's visions were to be *read*, and so would achieve their effect through a literary medium. (North says 'read silently'; but all the available evidence suggests that reading in the ancient world implied reading aloud).

Wherever precisely Zechariah is to be placed on the line of development from prophecy to apocalyptic, there can be no doubt that one point which binds him into the prophetic tradition is the affinity between him and Ezekiel. As has already been noted, one way in which that affinity has been expressed is by the suggestion that they both represent a particular socio-religious group within the community which can be identified over against other groups. That proposal will be considered more fully in the next chapter. But there are in any case clear links with Ezekiel which remain striking whatever judgment may be passed on that particular thesis. Not the least of these links is the common use of visionary material of a kind which both needs detailed interpretation before its meaning becomes clear and also uses the literary device of an angelic intermediary to establish this meaning. In Ezekiel 40-48 the interpreter is simply described as 'a/the man' (Ezek. 40.3, 4, etc.); but his role and function are clearly closely comparable with those of 'the angel who talked with me' in Zechariah (1.9 etc.). The importance of the Jerusalem temple provides a further link between Ezekiel and Zechariah, and so also does their common concern for the priesthood. Ezekiel 44 spells out in detail the need for a properly purified priesthood as the basis for ministry in the new temple which is envisaged, and the vision of Joshua in Zechariah 3 provides a specific illustration of the same concerns, applied to a particular individual.

The significance of these similarities is often challenged on the grounds that whereas Ezekiel is a visionary, giving a blueprint for a temple which was never in fact built, in Zechariah there is a more pragmatic concern rooted in the political realities of the contemporary situation. There may be some truth in this; judgment is rendered more difficult by the uncertainty about the relationship of Ezekiel 40-48 to the material in the earlier part of that book, and its dating. But we ought not to fall into the error of supposing that 'visionary' implies 'divorced from everyday reality'. Zechariah too was a visionary, and both in Zechariah and in Ezekiel 40-48 we see, alongside the visionary presentation, great concern for the precise practical details in which the truth of the vision was to be worked out.

Zechariah thus stands at an important point in the development of Israel's perception of God's word. There may be a sense in which the new outburst of prophetic activity about 520 BC marked an attempt to restore the old traditions of the nation-state, but that seems more characteristic of Haggai than of Zechariah. With Zechariah the prominence of the visions suggests rather that new modes of understanding God's dealings with his people are coming to the fore. In that sense, therefore, the editorial viewpoint in 1.4-6, which seems to differentiate Zechariah from 'the former prophets', is justified; similarly the universal vision of 8. 20-23 points forward to a situation in which a religious community will be able to express its beliefs in a way which is scarcely possible for a nation-state.

So far we have paid attention almost exclusively to the visions in Zechariah 1-6, and chs. 7-8 have simply been regarded as part of the editorial 'framework'. It is, however, important to notice that these chapters by no means consist simply of comment on or clarification of the visions. They raise a further question: Fasting. This theme provides the structure (7.1-7; 8.18f.) around which the editorial comments, with their repeated 'says the LORD of Hosts', have been elaborated in the remainder of these chapters.

Traditionally this section dealing with fasting has been understood as showing that Zechariah's oracles led to the abandonment of the customary fasts, not only that about which enquiry was made (7.3) but also three other fasts (8.19). The most common understanding of this section is to suppose that Zechariah was condemning the people for their obsession with outward practice and insisting that there were inner aspects of religion ('Render true judgments, show kindness and mercy' etc., 7.9f.) more important than fasting. This would then be closely comparable with the attacks on the cult found in the pre-exilic prophets, and in particular with the section on true fasting in Isaiah 58. Recently, however, R.E. Friedman has pointed out, in an article entitled 'The Prophet and the Historian', that this interpretation is very alien to the general character of Zechariah's message. Nowhere else is he pictured as one who condemns false religious practice; his emphasis was on comfort and hope for a community restoring its religious norms. Friedman therefore suggests that the section dealing with the abandonment of fasts should be seen as a picture of an ideal future, 'a time of joy and gladness in which the fasts will disappear' (v. 11).

There is force in Friedman's objection to the traditional view, though his reassessment is not without precedent (cf. the discussion in Petersen's commentary, 284-96, 312-15, and the references there given). For our immediate concern we may notice that the two interpretations roughly correspond to the two views of Zechariah. One places him in the long-established prophetic tradition, as may be suggested by the text itself (7.12); the other is evocative of that conviction about God's future work on his people's behalf that is associated with the later apocalypses. Here again we see in Zechariah something of a bridge between prophecy and apocalyptic. It is to the placing of Zechariah within the developing social setting of his time that we must now turn.

Further Reading

As with Haggai (see previous chapter) the appropriate starting-point is the various commentaries: all those listed there deal also with Zechariah 1-8. (D.W. Thomas supplied the commentary on Zechariah 1-8 as well as that on Haggai for the *Interpreter's Bible*). The brief notes on the commentaries are broadly applicable also to those on Zechariah. Ackroyd's study is also relevant to Zechariah (*Exile and Restoration*, ch. 11).

Among articles on these chapters the following should be noted particularly:

R.E. Friedman, 'The Prophet and the Historian: the Acquisition of Historical Information from Literary Sources' in R.E. Friedman, ed., *The Poet and the Historian* (Harvard Semitic Studies 26), Chico: Scholars Press, 1983, 1-12.

R. North, 'Prophecy to Apocalyptic via Zechariah', *SVT 22*, 1972, 47-71.

D.L. Petersen, 'Zechariah's Visions: a Theological Perspective', *VT* 34 (1984), 195-206.

6

'PARTIES' IN THE
RELIGIOUS
COMMUNITY?

ONE OF THE CONCERNS of Old Testament scholarship in recent years has been an attempt to probe behind the recorded words of the prophets, and to explore more precisely the social and political milieux in which those prophets should be sought. There is a good deal of dispute whether such an exercise can escape the inherent danger of arguing in a circle, since we have no independent evidence which can act as a control upon our findings relating to the political and social structure of ancient Israel. Such uncertainties have not prevented the attempt from being made, and in particular the situation of the restored community in the late sixth century BC and the role of the prophets in that community have attracted a good deal of discussion.

Two books in particular should be mentioned at this point: O. Plöger, *Theokratie und Eschatologie* (1959), translated into English as *Theocracy and Eschatology* (1968); and P.D. Hanson, *The Dawn of Apocalyptic* (1975). Each attempts to establish that there existed within the community parties which understood God's dealings with his people in significantly different ways. In particular they argue that the prophetic material from this period offers evidence of such different understandings. (A third book which shares something of the same approach, and has evoked even greater controversy, is Morton Smith, *Palestinian Parties and Politics that shaped the Old Testament* [New York and London: Columbia University Press, 1971]; but this need not concern us here so directly, as the role of Haggai and Zechariah is not a particularly important part of its thesis.)

The reader of the books by Plöger and Hanson will not gain a very favourable impression of Haggai and Zechariah. Though the thesis put forward by the two scholars differs in certain important respects, it is still in essence the same. It maintains that the post-exilic prophets can be divided into two groups. For Plöger, the differentiation is to be seen essentially in theological terms: it is a difference between 'theocracy' and 'eschatology'. The former embodied the understanding of those who saw the rule of God as operative in the existing situation, and so not to be questioned. The eschatologists, on the other hand, nourished a vision of a future in which the sad limitations of the contemporary state of affairs would be overcome.

Hanson pursued this point further by attempting to place the prophets who held such views in specific social and political contexts. For Hanson the real depth, the genuine insight, into what God had done for his people in the past and might be expected to do again in the future lay with the authors of Isaiah 40–66, the 'visionaries', as he called them. But these were excluded from real power and decision-making within the community. Those prerogatives were being exercised by such men as Haggai and Zechariah. In contrast with the glowing idealism of the authors of Isaiah 40–66, these are pictured by Hanson in essentially negative terms as men of limited vision, eager to cling to the position into which they had manoeuvred themselves. They were strengthened by their established position within the Jerusalem community and by their involvement with the worship of the temple, which enabled them to portray their opponents as outsiders. (Hanson deals particularly with Haggai and Zechariah 1–8 on pp. 240-62. Something of his attitude towards Haggai and Zechariah can be caught by his references on p. 247 to 'the ignominious path upon which the prophetic office was sent by Haggai and Zechariah'. These, he says, 'placed prophecy in the uncritical service of a specific political system' and gave up 'the revolutionary element which was always an essential ingredient in genuine prophecy'.)

These are harsh criticisms; and it will be necessary to consider whether or not they are justified. First of all, however, it is important that Hanson's work in general should be recognized for its positive value. It represents a serious attempt to supply a plausible sociological and political context for the literature of a period about which our ignorance remains great, and any future approach will have to supply an alternative reconstruction if anything of the same impact is to be achieved. (For a detailed consideration of Hanson's work, including an extended résumé of his main thesis, see

R.P. Carroll, 'Twilight of Prophecy or Dawn of Apocalyptic?', *JSOT* 14 [1979], 3-35.)

That being said, it remains true that it is the treatment of Haggai and Zechariah 1-8 which is probably the least satisfactory feature of Hanson's reconstruction. (It is important to emphasize that in the case of Zechariah it is only chs. 1-8 which are the subject of Hanson's strictures: he regards chs. 9-14 as part of the 'visionary' material.) There is, as is widely acknowledged, a general problem concerning the difficulty of making any kind of objective sociological assessment of biblical or any other ancient literary material. In addition to this two points need to be made concerning Hanson's approach.

First, his manner of arranging the material hides very important but unstated assumptions. These are: (a) the presupposition that Isaiah 56-66 are contemporary with Haggai and Zechariah. In fact there is no consensus regarding the date of this material, and all kinds of proposals have been made. (b) It is by no means self-evident that the existence of two such contemporary bodies of prophetic material—allowing that they *are* roughly contemporary—means that they must be regarded as in opposition to one another: the Old Testament provides numerous examples of apparently contemporary prophetic collections, without any kind of cross-reference to suggest that they should be so understood (e.g. Amos and Hosea; Jeremiah and Ezekiel, not to mention minor prophets such as Nahum and Habakkuk who are not so easily dated). More generally (c) in his legitimate enthusiasm for the vision and insight of Isaiah 40-66 Hanson seems to assume that support for one group must entail denigration of others, as if they were no more than obstacles in the way of the true vision reaching fulfilment. As is shown by the above quotation from his book, Hanson's negative approach to Haggai and Zechariah is more reminiscent of an advocate pleading a case than of a scholar attempting an impartial assessment of the evidence; and the books so dismissed are given little opportunity to speak for themselves.

Secondly—and this is of even more direct relevance—such a characterization of Haggai and Zechariah plays down a very important aspect of their message. They are regarded by Hanson as solely concerned with immediate needs, 'tying the prophetic word to a particular political officialdom and a specific political program' (*Dawn of Apocalyptic*, 247). Only thus, it is suggested, could they safeguard their own privileged position. But in fact there is an important eschatological element in the words of each of these prophets which ought to be given due weight. To Haggai the building of the temple was of supreme importance, but it was not an end in itself: it was a means to an even more important end. As we have already seen, the climax of the book (2.20-23) is an expectation of what will happen 'on that day'. Some great event is to be anticipated, pictured as the shaking of heavens and earth and the overthrow of the thrones of kingdoms. Yet this passage is ignored by Hanson, who concentrates exclusively on those sections of the book which are concerned with 'the ushering in of the blessings tied to the temple program' (*Dawn*, 175). If we are to do justice to Haggai, it is important to recognize both the significance he attached to the restoration of the temple and the way in which that was to be the prelude to even greater acts by God on behalf of his people. We might conclude, from the modest subsequent history of the community, that Haggai was wrong in his expectations; but we cannot in all fairness accuse him of lack of any such anticipation.

The same is true to an even greater extent with Zechariah. We may at once feel that there is a certain irony in contrasting Zechariah with 'the visionaries', given the nature of his own prophetic experience. It is undeniable that there are difficulties in interpreting the message of Zechariah, precisely because it is couched in visionary terms. Nevertheless it seems clear that his range of expectation extended significantly beyond the immediate concerns of the Jerusalem community. Thus whereas Hanson dismisses the visions of Zechariah as 'propaganda for the Zadokite temple program' (we may note in passing that there is no reference to Zadok or Zadokites anywhere in Zechariah!), it is surely appropriate to look also for their wider concerns. Thus 2.1-5, with its description of the 'measuring' of Jerusalem, shows far more than a mere concern for the correct restoration of the city: the divine presence symbolized in v. 5, with its allusion to the imagery of the Exodus ('a wall of fire round about') and to the 'glory' tradition best known from Ezekiel, but having much more ancient roots, is to be a continuing feature of the renewed community. (On Zechariah's use of the 'glory' tradition, see T.N.D. Mettinger, *The Dethronement of Sabaoth*, Lund: Gleerup, especially 114f., where he speaks of Zechariah as one who 'harks back to "classical" terminology'.) Comparable points can be made with regard to the other visions in Zechariah 1-8.

Another aspect of Hanson's analysis of the structure of the community which may properly evoke caution is his proposed typology. His book is entitled *The Dawn of Apocalyptic*, and an important part of his purpose is to trace the relation between prophecy and apocalyptic. Apocalyptic has often been described as 'the child of prophecy'; is it possible to be more precise about the nature of that parentage? (This particular metaphor, of the parent/child relation, is much used by Hanson, and is spelt out in great detail in the final chapter of his book, called 'An Allegory and its Explication' [402-13].) For Hanson the route from prophecy to apocalyptic lay by way of Isaiah 40–55 (characterized as 'Proto-Apocalyptic'), through Isaiah 56–66 ('Early Apocalyptic'), and then via Zechariah 9–14 to the fully developed apocalypses of later ages. But it is noteworthy that quite different typologies have been proposed: North, for example, as we have noted, took the route to have been 'Prophecy to Apocalyptic via Zechariah', and in the same volume a short article by S. Amsler, 'Zacharie et l'Origine de l'Apocalyptique' (*SVT* 22, 227-31) also argues for the pivotal role of Zechariah 1–8 in the development of apocalyptic on the grounds of the changed view of history discernible in these chapters.

It would seem, therefore, that two rather different issues have been brought together in discussion, and in a fashion which can prove somewhat misleading. On the one hand there is the mainly *sociological* quest, the attempt to isolate different and possibly competing social groups within the restored community of Judaism. On the other hand there is a *literary* concern, attempting to identify certain characteristic features of the prophetic and apocalyptic writings, and to deduce from them how the transition from one to the other is most appropriately understood. Two recent survey-articles, each with its own original contribution to offer, have discussed these issues. Both are somewhat marginal to the study of Haggai and Zechariah 1–8, but they are of great value in helping the student to see the larger context of the Judaism of the Second Temple period. They are: E.W. Nicholson, 'Apocalyptic', in G.W. Anderson (ed.), *Tradition and Interpretation*, Oxford: Clarendon Press, 1979, 189-213 (an article largely concerned with the relation between prophecy and apocalyptic); and M.A. Knibb, 'Prophecy and the Emergence of the Jewish Apocalypses', in Coggins, Phillips and Knibb, *Israel's Prophetic Tradition*, 155-80 (the first and third sections of this article, dealing with potential confusions in terminology and with possible modes of development from prophecy to the apocalypses, are especially relevant).

Reverting now to the basic theme of this chapter, the 'placing' of Haggai and Zechariah within the overall social structure of the emerging Jewish community, it seems that Hanson's assessment has the effect of forcing them into an alien role which there is not sufficient evidence to sustain, either from the books themselves or comparatively by way of a contrast with the later chapters of Isaiah. We should probably be wise to admit that we have insufficient evidence to enable us to spell out the detailed structure of the community. This is true in general; with specific reference to Haggai and Zechariah we need also to bear in mind the points made in Chapter 3, that their words have been edited in such a way as to present a picture significantly different from that of their own time.

The fact remains, of course, that from a later period we have evidence of a much less ambiguous kind for the divisions within the Jewish community: the New Testament, the Dead Sea Scrolls, and the literary survivals from the period of the Maccabee uprising all in their different ways illustrate this. In the other work mentioned at the beginning of this chapter, Plöger concentrates his attention on this later material; and although he recognizes, and attempts to trace the development of, the theocratic and eschatological viewpoint in some pre-second-century material, his concern does not really stretch back to the period of Haggai and Zechariah. This may be wise. Though there were no doubt differences within the community of their day, the evidence does not allow us to engage in precise analysis, nor does it enable us to say whether those differences correspond to the theocratic and eschatological emphases of a later period.

We may end this chapter (and in effect our discussion of Haggai and Zechariah 1–8) with two additional comments. The first concerns the relation of Zechariah to apocalyptic modes of expression. It is clearly the case that Zechariah 1–8 contains many literary features which are characteristic of the later apocalypses: visions, the role of interpreting angels, numerical symbolism, animal represent-ation as embodying particular symbolical realities. We have seen already that this must certainly raise doubts about Zechariah's being legitimately seen as representative of a group whose overriding concern was the maintenance of good order and the establishment of satisfactory relations with the imperial authorities. But the question must also be raised: does the presence of these literary features make it legitimate to describe these chapters as apocalyptic, or should they simply be regarded as one development of the prophetic tradition? Sharply differing answers have been given to this question. At one extreme, L.G. Rignell, *Die Nachtgesichte des Sacharja* (Lund: Gleerup, 1950) placed Zechariah wholly within the 'classical' prophetic tradition, while a very different approach has been taken more recently by H. Gese, notably in an article 'Anfang und Ende der Apokalyptik dargestellt am Sacharjabuch' (*ZThK*, 1973, 20-49), which, as the title implies, sees the whole course of the development of apocalyptic from beginning to end exhibited in the book of Zechariah.

As is so often the case with differences of this kind, it is not likely that one scholar will simply be right and another wrong. Much depends on the terms of reference and the definitions that are introduced. If the attempt is to be made (as by Hanson) to penetrate behind the literary form of the material and discover something of the political and social context from which the apocalypses emerged, then this will in turn clearly affect our literary classification. So, for Hanson, the eschatological element which he regards as essential for a true apocalypse is lacking in Zechariah. If, on the other hand, such an attempt is either regarded as impossible or is considered irrelevant, then (as to some extent with Gese) the particular focus of attention will be the literary features of a book, and in that respect Zechariah 1-8 may certainly be judged as true apocalyptic. In fact, Gese is more willing than some scholars to take social and political matters into consideration. For him, the fact that Zechariah was a member of a priestly family is significant, suggesting that apocalyptic was not a literary form that developed among the 'outsiders' (as proposed by Hanson), but one that emerged from within the ranks of the establishment itself.

Gese's title refers to the *book* of Zechariah, that is, the whole of chs. 1-14, and this leads to the second additional point that needs to be made in the present context. We have assumed thus far that chs. 9-14 stand apart from chs. 1-8, and in the next chapter some of the reasons for that conclusion will be discussed. Nevertheless, for Hanson's thesis to stand, 9-14 would need to be completely detached from 1-8, for he regards the later chapters as the product of the visionary school which was set in sharp opposition to the theocratic establishment. But though there are indeed considerable and important differences between the two sections, they have been joined so as to form one book, and it is difficult to see why or how this should have taken place if they originally represented directly opposed points of view. It is to the problems associated with Zechariah 9-14 that we must now direct our attention.

Further Reading

The relevant material for this particular point of issue has been mentioned in the body of the chapter; what is set out below is simply more precise bibliographical information. The two particular proponents of a 'party' split as a key to our understanding of Second Temple Judaism are:

O. Plöger, *Theocracy and Eschatology*, Oxford: Blackwell, 1968 (more important for the general statement of the thesis than for direct consideration of Haggai and Zechariah 1-8, but Zechariah 12-14 are discussed in detail, 78-96).

P.D. Hanson, *The Dawn of Apocalyptic*, Philadelphia: Fortress, 2nd edn, 1979 (ch. 3, 209-79, deals with the 'hierocracy'; the detailed discussion of Haggai and Zechariah 1-8 is section E, 240-62. Zechariah 9-14 are regarded as from a radically opposed viewpoint, and are dealt with in ch. 4).

For discussion of Hanson (in particular) and Plöger, see:

R.P. Carroll, 'Twilight of Prophecy or Dawn of Apocalyptic?', *JSOT* (1979), 3-35.

R. Mason, 'The Prophets of the Restoration' and M.A. Knibb, 'The Emergence of the Jewish Apocalypses', in Coggins, Phillips and Knibb, *Israel's Prophetic Tradition*, especially 137-42, 169-76.

On the legitimacy (or otherwise) of describing Zech. 1-8 as 'apocalyptic', see (in addition to the discussion in Knibb's article above):

D.S. Russell, *The Method and Message of Jewish Apocalyptic*, London: SCM Press, 1964, especially 88-91 (a standard textbook, now somewhat dated, but a clear statement of traditional views).

R. North, 'Prophecy to Apocalyptic via Zechariah', *SVT 22*, Leiden: Brill, 1972, 47-71.

7

ZECHARIAH 9–14

A RECENT REVIEW of D.L. Petersen's commentary, *Haggai and Zechariah 1–8*, welcomes it as a 'distinguished' piece of work, but goes on to express surprise 'that anyone in these days should write a commentary that ends at ch. 8' (C.S. Rodd, 'Talking Points from Books', *ExpT* 96 [1985], 260). It may be helpful to consider the implications of this comment as an introduction to our discussion of Zechariah 9–14.

An appropriate starting-point is a comparison with the book of Isaiah. For something like 200 years the consensus of critical scholarship has been that the material from ch. 40 to the end of the book of Isaiah cannot come from the eighth-century prophet Isaiah ben-Amoz; and so it is a commonplace to speak of 'Deutero- or Second-Isaiah' when referring to chs. 40–55, and, less commonly, of 'Trito- or Third-Isaiah' when referring to chs. 56–66. As will shortly be seen, the book of Zechariah, although this has attracted less attention, has been divided by critical scholars in a comparable way, with the first part (1–8) containing a nucleus of material going back to Zechariah himself, though with extensive editorial elaborations, and the remainder of the book, which cannot be attributed to Zechariah or his immediate circle, consisting of two collections, chs. 9–11 and 12–14. It has thus become customary to think of 'Deutero-' and 'Trito-Zechariah'.

But just at the time when the division of the book of Isaiah has come to be accepted among scholars of a quite conservative standpoint and even in some English versions (cf. the introduction to Isaiah in the *Good News Bible*), a great deal of attention has begun to be paid to the sense in which the book of Isaiah *is* nevertheless a unity, even though its various elements come from widely differing periods. Despite its diversity in terms of historical origin, the book of

Isaiah has been brought into its present shape *as a unity*. Such is now the view of many modern scholars who are very far removed from that fundamentalist approach which insists that the whole of Isaiah consists of the words of a single prophet. The question naturally arises—and is implicit in the reviewer's comment quoted at the beginning of this chapter—whether a similar unity can be detected in the book of Zechariah.

It is clear, then, that there are several important questions about Zechariah 9-14 which demand consideration even before any attention is given to its specific contents. In this chapter we shall need to consider four related but distinct topics: first, the reasons why these chapters are very widely regarded as coming from a background different from that of chs. 1-8; secondly, their possible historical setting, or other clues as to their origin; thirdly, the question whether they have been deliberately linked with chs. 1-8 to form a coherent book, or are simply a block of anonymous material added to the existing collection; and fourthly, some points of interpretative detail that arise within the material. One disclaimer must be made at the outset: the sheer variety of the theories that have been put forward concerning Zechariah 9-14 will necessitate an even more selective discussion than elsewhere in this volume. At the same time it must be stressed that it would be quite misleading to dismiss these chapters as of little significance: one need only look at their importance in shaping the Gospel accounts of the Passion of Jesus to see how creative a part they came to play.

1. The Separation of Zechariah 9-14 from 1-8

The grounds for separating chs. 9-14 from 1-8 have been correctly summarized by Baldwin as centring 'round three main issues: contents, style, vocabulary' (*Commentary*, 62). The difference in contents is obvious even at the first glance. The series of visions comes to an end, and references to the restoration of the Jerusalem community and its temple in the reign of Darius are no longer to be found. The Jewish leaders, Joshua and Zerubbabel, are not mentioned. In chs. 1-8 the prophet Zechariah is mentioned by name four times and the 'I' of the visions is clearly identified with him. By contrast the oracles in 9-14 are anonymous, and set out in a markedly different style from the visions of the first section. Though both sections have claims to a significant place in the development towards apocalyptic, they are certainly not identical in this respect. Finally, there are considerable differences in vocabulary, both with regard to the occurrence of particular characteristic expressions in one part but not the other, and in detailed word-usage. (The fullest discussion of this is in Mitchell, especially 236.)

Such differences between the two parts of the book created uncertainties about the status of chs. 9–14 from very early times. These may be said, in a sense, to go back to the New Testament: Matt. 27.9 quotes the reference in Zech. 11.12f. to the thirty pieces of silver, but attributes the quotation to Jeremiah. This may be a simple mistake, or a confusion with passages in Jeremiah in which similar themes are treated. It is scarcely likely that Zechariah 11 was at some point in antiquity actually attributed to Jeremiah, though such a view became fashionable at one time and effectively represents the first questioning of the authorship of these chapters. In the seventeenth century Joseph Mede of Cambridge put forward the suggestion that the Holy Spirit guided Matthew to correct the false attribution of these chapters to Zechariah in Jewish tradition. (The early history of controversy on these chapters is reviewed in the commentary by R.L. Smith, but in a somewhat confusing way, since the main facts are set out twice [169-73 in the general introduction to Zechariah, 242-49 in the introduction to Zechariah 9–14] and a number of details repeated, some with inaccurate dates and references.) This original suggestion led the way to a great variety of proposals concerning chs. 9–14, the most important of which we must now briefly note.

2. The Origin and Historical Setting of Zechariah 9–14

In addition to the supposition that the Gospel of Matthew might provide a clue to the origin of these chapters, another inner-biblical pointer was fastened upon as a possible guide. In 1.1 Zechariah is described as 'the son of Berechiah'. In the earlier discussion of Zechariah 1–8 in this book (p. 44) it was suggested that this might best be seen as a redactional device, linking this Zechariah with the 'Zechariah the son of Jeberechiah' of Isa. 8.2. But that is, of course, a characteristic twentieth-century, redaction-critical proposal. At an earlier period it was proposed that the Zechariah of Isaiah's time might have been the author of these chapters, and that through a misunderstanding they had been grouped with the words of the later

Zechariah. This would not only explain the apparent 'error' in 1.1, but would also account for the fact that chs. 9–11 in particular seem to reflect a certain kinship with the oracles of the pre-exilic prophets (e.g. 10.1f., with its denunciation of idolatry, which could be compared with the attacks on cultic worship found in the eighth-century prophets), and that they apparently reflect the historical enemies of the pre-exilic period rather than of any later time (e.g. 10.11, where the overthrow of Assyria and Egypt is predicted).

It would be difficult to find a modern scholar who holds the view that these chapters are simply the work of a pre-exilic prophet; but a modification of that understanding which has found some favour is that in these chapters an anthology of earlier oracles has been edited at a late period, as part of the interpretative process which was characteristic of the attitude of the Judaism of the Greek period to its earlier traditions. (This view is set out in the 'Introduction to the Prophets' in the *Jerusalem Bible*, 1139, where these chapters are described as 'a disorderly collection of possibly ancient passages'.)

Such a view has, however, seemed to many to raise unnecessary complications, and so for the last century the dominant critical hypothesis has been that first put forward by B. Stade in a series of studies published in the 1880s, that 'Deutero-Zechariah' (the term he used, and the one which has come into common usage, partly on the analogy with 'Deutero-Isaiah') should be dated entirely in the Greek period, more precisely the late fourth or early third century. Stade took the six chapters to be a unity; and although this point has been much disputed, his general thesis as to date and probable setting has been that most generally followed—though, it must be confessed, this often appears to be for lack of any convincing alternative. In fact all the supposed allusions to dates and historical situations are so vague and imprecise that there is little likelihood of general agreement, and as a result this approach to the material has been abandoned by many scholars.

No single alternative approach can in any sense be said to have established itself as more satisfactory. Here we shall briefly note three different types of understanding which have been put forward, choosing them at least in part in order to illustrate the wide variety of approaches which have been suggested.

The first of these to be considered is a literary study. Though the work of P. Lamarche, *Zacharie IX-XIV: Structure littéraire et messianisme* (Paris: Gabalda), appeared as long ago as 1961, it represents an approach to much Old Testament material which has flourished in more recent times.

Basically, Lamarche saw an indication of single authorship in these chapters in an elaborate chiastic pattern running through them. There is no doubt that chiasmus (at its simplest, an a:b:b:a structure within a literary unit) was a regularly used literary form in ancient Israel; whether anything so elaborate as that proposed by Lamarche for Zechariah 9-14 is probable is another matter. He saw the chapters as beginning and ending (9.1-8; 14.16-21) with the announcement of judgment and salvation for the nations surrounding Israel. Such a device, of beginning and ending sections with similar material, is known as *inclusio*, and it may fairly be seen here. Much more problematic is Lamarche's argument relating to the intervening sections, where he claimed to detect recurring references to the king of Israel and to the war and victory of Israel over her enemies, together with the attacks upon idolatry, all set out in an identifiable pattern. Objective proof of theories of this kind is notoriously difficult to achieve; most reviewers and commentators have been reserved in their judgments. Among the most enthusiastic supporters of this view of the structure of Zechariah 9-14 has been Baldwin; her commentary provides a clear and sympathetic statement of this type of approach, with a chart illustrating Lamarche's proposals (75-81).

A literary understanding of this kind almost by definition excludes precise judgments as to date or historical setting. There is, however, one link to the second type of approach which we shall now consider. The second half of Lamarche's title shows that he regards one of the themes of this literary unit to be an exposition of messianic belief; and in the last part of his book he sets out his own view of the way in which the references to the king of Israel are best understood. In these chapters the development of messianic understanding is in effect a kind of commentary upon, and development of, the Servant passages in Isaiah 40-55. Such a view has been accepted by some of those who have not agreed with Lamarche in his literary analysis; it supplies a link with our second type of approach.

This is best exemplified by Mason. In his commentary (79) he notes that a 'general characteristic of these chapters is their dependence on earlier biblical material, especially, but not exclusively, on the major prophetic writings of the Old Testament'. He notes that earlier scholars had been aware of this phenomenon; and indeed

Mitchell in his commentary supplied a list of such passages (237f.). (A curiosity, and a reminder of the subjective aspect of this kind of study, lies in the fact that Mitchell's list makes no mention of the passage regarded by Mason as the clearest example of such dependence: the relationship between Zechariah 13.5 and Amos 7.14.)

The particular importance of this type of approach lies in the fact that it shows how a new attitude towards earlier prophetic writings had developed. These had now come to be regarded as 'holy writings', needing interpretation and explanation. If this type of approach were generally adopted and developed, it would reinforce the scepticism towards the mainly historical method of interpretation of these chapters to which we have referred above. For example, it has frequently been argued that behind the description of a conqueror in 9.1-8 it is possible to see allusions to the triumphant progress of Alexander the Great through Palestine. But if this passage were to be understood as an exegesis of the denunciation of Tyre in Ezekiel 28, the precise historical reference to Alexander would become much more problematic. In short, such an approach to these chapters is to see in them a precursor of the kind of commentary found in the Dead Sea Scrolls, where great importance is attached to commentary upon, and application of, prophetic writings. (The 'Habakkuk Commentary', among the first scrolls to be discovered, is still the clearest example of the genre.) If this kind of understanding is acceptable, it would suggest that Zechariah 9-14 represent a very late addition to the main body of the Prophets made when interest in them as holy writings was already growing.

For this kind of approach the present placing of these chapters, within the book of Zechariah, is in effect coincidental: they are not linked with Zechariah 1-8 in any direct way. The third approach which we are to consider, on the other hand, supposes the existence of a much closer relationship. Gese, in the article already cited, was concerned with the whole book of Zechariah. He maintained that the night visions in Zechariah 1-8 are the oldest apocalypse known to us, and that to them have been added further collections of apocalyptic material: the first in chs. 9-11, with its particular messianic emphasis and the second in 12-14, where the stress is rather on what was later to be called martyrdom. In both of these aspects Zechariah provides a significant link between the prophetic tradition and the book of Daniel. This approach also (and this is an important aspect of Gese's thesis) rules out those theories which make apocalyptic a product of wisdom schools (so von Rad), or of an 'anti-establishment' group (so Plöger), or of Jewish reaction to Iranian or Hellenistic influence (so many earlier scholars).

The issue of the relationship between chs. 1–8 and 9–14 will occupy us further in our next section; here we may simply note that the differing starting-points of the three theories which have been briefly outlined here enable their proponents to arrive at very different conclusions. According to whether we concentrate on the literary structure with Lamarche, on the interpretative links with earlier Old Testament material with Mason, or on the development towards apocalyptic with Gese, different aspects of this material will naturally be regarded as providing the key to the interpretation of the whole. In principle, it is clear that we should be one stage nearer to resolving problems of this kind if it were possible to decide in what sense the book in its present form may be regarded as a unity; and it is to that question that we must now turn.

3. The Shape of the Book of Zechariah

The scholar who more than anyone else has brought the issue of the final canonical shape of the various books of the Old Testament into prominence is B.S. Childs, and so it is with his assessment of the final form of the book of Zechariah that we may conveniently begin. He rightly notes that there are certain links between chapters 1–8 and 9–14, though these are for the most part thematic rather than precise verbal links, and are of the kind that might be expected from any two Jerusalemite prophetic collections. He concludes this brief discussion (in *Introduction to the Old Testament as Scripture*, 482f.) with the further remark that 'the case for compatibility of content between the first and second parts of the book should not be overstated'. He therefore acknowledges that 'the canonical process which resulted in shaping the book of Zechariah was of a very different order than that which fashioned the Isaianic corpus' (480), and he goes on to make various—admittedly tentative—suggestions concerning this process. In the end, however, the most specific suggestion which he makes is concerned with our perception of the book of Zechariah within the larger Old Testament canon rather than with any more precise proposal about the shaping of the book of Zechariah itself. This suggestion is that Zechariah 9–14 provides an important link between Zechariah 1-8 and Daniel; this insight, however, does not appear to be dependent upon any particular theory of canonical form.

In one respect the links of these chapters are with what follows rather than with what precedes. In Zech. 9.1, 12.1 and Mal. 1.1 the opening phrase is identical: 'An oracle; the word of the LORD . . .' (RSV renders the expression slightly differently in Mal. 1.1, but in the Hebrew the wording is identical with that of the others). This fact has given rise to the suggestion that this phrase serves to introduce three blocks of anonymous prophetic material which have been added to round off the Book of the Twelve and indeed the whole prophetic canon. (This view was put forward as at least a partial explanation of the problem by Eissfeldt, *The Old Testament: an Introduction* [Oxford: Blackwell, 1965], 440; he recognized, however, that this feature is no more than a contribution by the final redactors of the material.) In fact the extreme diversity of the material which follows these introductions is such that no real understanding of the contents of Zechariah 9-14 and Malachi is offered thereby. Indeed, so great is that diversity that some attention must be paid to it in our consideration of the shape of the book. Whereas Zechariah 1-8 has clearly definable structure, here we are confronted with bewildering variety.

To begin at the end, which somehow seems appropriate when studying Zechariah, we may note first of all that ch. 14 stands somewhat apart from what precedes; Rudolph, for example, excludes it from his consideration of the main body of Zechariah 9-14 as being a wholly distinct unit, a vision of the fate of Jerusalem at the end-time (*Commentary*, 161); other scholars, on the other hand (Childs, p. 481, is one example), claim that chs. 12-14 form a unit linked by the series of introductory formulas 'in that day'. Even Childs, however, admits that 13.7-9 form an exception to this general judgment, and it is noteworthy that this passage is transposed in NEB to follow 11.17, to which it is linked both in form (poetry) and in theme (the attack upon the unworthy shepherds). Thus, what Lamarche and others have seen as evidence of a deliberate structure is here taken as showing that there has been displacement of the proper order—a classic example of the varied judgments which competent scholars have arrived at when confronted with the same evidence. In any case, we may note that the close links between 13.7-9 and the 'shepherd' material in ch. 11, whether or not the present order is changed, make it unlikely that we should think of a 'Trito-Zechariah' independently responsible for chs. 12–14.

So far it would seem most likely that chs. 9–14 represent one or more blocks of varied material added to the words of Zechariah with little apparent attempt to integrate the whole into an ordered book. Is there any evidence which points in the other direction and suggests a greater coherence in the whole book?

The very most that can be said in this respect is that it seems unlikely that the juxtaposing of 9–14 with 1–8 is purely a matter of chance. Though as we have already noted there are links between Zech. 9.1, 12.1 and Mal. 1.1 which suggest that the three collections have been shaped in a deliberately similar way, this similarity does not extend to the contents of the material. In other words, as far as we are able to trace, Zechariah 9–14 have always been accepted as belonging with Zechariah 1–8 rather than as standing on their own or with Malachi. There are enough similarities of general theme to demonstrate this: what Childs (482) describes as 'a surprising compatibility between the two books [*sic*: this must surely be a misprint for 'blocks'] of material'. In other words, this was not a purely arbitrary joining of unrelated prophetic oracles. Among the 'elements of congruity' (again the phrase is Childs's) to be noted are: common reflection upon earlier authoritative religious traditions; concern for the renewal of Jerusalem; judgment on, and conversion of, the nations; a glorious future under the rule of a 'messianic' figure.

An analogous approach is to be found in another article by Mason, 'The Relation of Zechariah 9–14 to Proto-Zechariah'. Here he examines five possible areas of similarity between the two bodies of material: the prominence of the Zion tradition, God's cleansing of the community, universalism, the appeal to earlier prophetic traditions, and the leadership of the community in the new age. In each of these areas Mason is able to detect lines of continuity (though, as we have already seen, his concluding comparison with Proto- and Deutero-Isaiah would not be universally allowed).

In summary, then, the links between the two parts of the book of Zechariah seem to be such as to rule out any suggestion of purely fortuitous juxtaposition. Nor is it easy to find evidence which would support Hanson's contention, in his reconstruction of the divided state of post-exilic Judaism, that Zechariah 1–8 must be placed in the theocratic camp and Zechariah 9–14 in the eschatological. Beyond that it is scarcely possible to go: evidence is simply insufficient for theories about the origin of these chapters to be more than speculative. The fact remains, however, that they have been of far greater importance in subsequent interpretation than this obscurity of origin might lead us to expect; and it is to that point that we must now turn.

4. The Interpretation of Zechariah 9–14

Reference has already been made to the way in which Matt. 27.9 quotes Zech. 11.12f. but attributes the passage to Jeremiah, and this can be our starting-point: the remarkably extensive use of these chapters in the New Testament, and especially in the Gospel passion-narratives. So we find that 9.9f. provide the scriptural basis for the account of Jesus' entry into Jerusalem on an ass. Matt. 21.4 specifies that 'this took place to fulfil what was spoken by the prophet', and the Gospel appears to misunderstand the nature of Hebrew poetic parallelism and so to have Jesus enter the city riding on two animals (21.7). In John 12.7 a substantially similar quotation from Zechariah is introduced by the standard mode of referring to the Old Testament: 'it is written'.

In addition to these references, Zech. 12.10 (RSV 'they look on him whom they have pierced', but the Hebrew is actually 'look on *me*'; cf. RV, NEB) is quoted in John 19.37 as 'another scripture' which is held to have prefigured the piercing of Jesus' body after his death on the cross. The meaning of the passage in its original context is widely disputed: some have sought an historical incident as its origin, others have supposed that some cultic ceremony is here referred to, while others again have seen here an elaboration of and commentary upon some earlier prophetic passage such as Ezek. 36.16-28. (The commentary of Lacocque offers a detailed discussion of this, 188-92.) Zech. 13.7, 'Strike the shepherd, that the sheep may be scattered', provides Matthew and Mark with the basis for their reference to the inevitable abandonment of Jesus by his disciples, a reference again introduced by the phrase 'it is written' (Matt. 26.31; Mark 14.27). Whatever other obscurities there may be, therefore, it is clear that these chapters played an important role for the early Christian community as proof-texts; it is unfortunate that there is little relevant evidence relating to these chapters from Qumran, so that we do not know whether the Dead Sea scrolls community made similar use of these or other passages.

It is not possible here to attempt exegesis of all the other uncertain passages in Zechariah 9-14, but some points are of particular importance. One such is the reference to the prophets in 13.2-6 to which allusion has already been made in an earlier chapter. Much depends on the interpretation of 13.5a, 'I am no prophet'. The Hebrew, *lō nābî ānōkî,* is identical with the celebrated passage in Amos 7.14; the question is whether the Zechariah passage is to be understood as a deliberate allusion to Amos, or whether the use of the same expression is purely coincidental. Many of the older commentaries take the latter view: this passage is taken by them to be a denunciation of a depraved form of prophecy whose exponents 'when it suits their interests . . . will not hesitate to lie, saying one and all, "I am not a prophet"' (Mitchell, 338). This would make this passage simply an illustration of the degradation into which prophecy fell. But most more recent commentators see a direct allusion to Amos, who (whatever his original intention) was seen as condemning the prophets of his day. At one level, that is to say, our passage is also a warning of the dangers of corruption inherent in even the best religious institutions.

One other important general point arises from this section. The next verse refers to 'these wounds on your back'. It might have been expected that either this phrase or the explanation of it in the next phrase, that they are 'the wounds I received in the house of my friends', would have been used by New Testament writers in their description of Christ's suffering. In fact they make no use of this passage, although it was a favourite of later Christian writers. More immediately relevant is the clue that this and v. 4, with its reference to a 'hairy mantle', may give us with regard to the outward manifestations of prophetism. The wounds may be seen as indications of the way in which prophets might work themselves up into an ecstatic frenzy; the mantle may have been a distinctive garment customarily worn by prophets. But the passage offers no support for any interpretation suggesting that the prophets here described were 'false' or 'professional' or 'Canaanite' prophets; what we have is a condemnation of prophets by a prophet such as is found frequently in the prophetic writings (e.g. Jer. 23.9-40).

The other theme in Zechariah 9-14 to which some brief attention must be given is that of the shepherds. This is a theme which runs right through chs. 10-11 and is found again in 13.7-9, a section which NEB has transposed from its context in the Hebrew Bible to a

position after ch. 11. For the most part the references to shepherds
are found in those denunciatory sections which are juxtaposed with
the hopeful elements in these chapters. It would be universally
agreed that the references to shepherds are figurative, and that the
word is a metaphor for ruler; this is common enough in the Old
Testament, whether the reference is to God himself (The LORD is my
shepherd, Ps. 23.1) or to his earthly vicegerent, the Davidic king (He
chose David his servant . . . to be the shepherd of Jacob his people,
Ps. 78.70f.). Here in Zechariah the references are clearly to earthly
leaders; the difficulty arises in deciding whether they are to be taken
as historical references which would in principle allow us to date
these oracles by possible historical allusions contained within them,
or whether they are better seen as interpretations of earlier biblical
passages along the same lines.

Again, as with the section on prophets, there has been a shift of
emphasis among commentators. The earlier custom was to attempt
to detect a specific historical situation in which these false 'shepherds'
were active in persecuting the faithful minority. In particular it was
because of supposed links with the oppression which culminated in
the crisis of the years 168-164 BC that these chapters were placed in
that period or the time leading up to it. (Mitchell regarded the
component elements of these chapters as coming from different parts
of the Greek period, on the basis of various supposed historical
allusions: *Commentary*, 251-59.) More recently, however, the
general tendency has been to acknowledge that such an historical
approach demands more detailed knowledge of events in the Greek
period than we can legitimately lay claim to, so that such an attempt
to pin down a precise historical setting is bound to be speculative. A
more instructive approach, it is now commonly argued, is to see in
these references the beginnings of a tradition of biblical commentary,
applying to the contemporary situation (whatever that may have
been) the warnings against false shepherds which are found
particularly in Jeremiah 25 and Ezekiel 34. Such an approach still
leaves many unsolved problems with regard to these chapters, but
does at least allow for our placing them within what was to be an
extremely important development in both Judaism and Christianity:
that is to say, they drew upon a body of early writings considered as
inspired, and attempted to interpret them in the light of the
circumstances of their own day. Something of the same process is at
work at least in the final form of the book of Malachi, to which we
must now turn.

Further Reading

The commentaries on Haggai (see the bibliography at the end of Chapter 4) all, with the exception of Petersen, deal with Zechariah 9–14 as well, and the comments made on them in the earlier bibliography remain relevant. (Petersen is to contribute a companion volume, on *Zechariah 9–14— Malachi*, to the SCM Press Old Testament Library series; this is likely to be published in 1987.)

Other relevant studies:

B.S. Childs, *Introduction*, 475-86.

R.A. Mason, 'The Relation of Zechariah 9-14 to Proto-Zechariah', *ZAW* 88 (1976), 226-39.

F.F. Bruce, 'The Book of Zechariah and the Passion Narrative', *BJRL* 43 (1961), 336-53.

D.R. Jones, 'A Fresh Interpretation of Zechariah ix-xi', *VT* 12 (1962), 241-59 (a different approach from those outlined above, proposing a situation for these chapters in the fifth century in Damascus and as the work of an exiled prophet who looked forward to the reunion of the scattered people under a Davidic ruler. This article is worthy of attention just because its views differ so markedly from other treatments of these chapters.)

8

MALACHI

THE OPENING WORDS of Malachi are, as we have already noted, identical with those of Zech. 9.1; 12.1; the closing words (4.5f.) also show some similarity with Zechariah in that they are concerned with the re-interpretation of earlier prophetic material. (These verses are numbered 4.5-6 in the English versions; but it should be noted that the Hebrew chapter division is different: 4.1-6 in the English are the equivalent of 3.19-24 in the Hebrew.) In the main body of material, however, we are in a world very different from that of Zechariah 9-14. In contrast with the visionary, allusive outlook of those chapters, we find here a very down-to-earth situation, with attacks upon kinds of current malpractice somewhat reminiscent of those condemned in earlier prophetic books.

In the critical introductions to the Old Testament two particular issues have dominated discussion of Malachi: authorship and date. We shall begin our consideration of the book with these.

Authorship

The point at issue here is whether or not 'Malachi' can rightly be understood as a proper name. It is generally agreed that its use in this way in 1.1 is a later editorial addition to the main collection of oracles and so of limited evidential value. But the word means 'my messenger'; and it is so used in 3.1 in a divine speech where it is most unlikely that a proper name is intended. As a proper name it is a possible though unusual form, and a few scholars (e.g. Baldwin, 211f.) accept it as such. The great majority of modern commentators, however, think it more likely that this collection of oracles was originally anonymous, and that the name 'Malachi' came to be regarded as a personal one at a later stage, perhaps when tradition had come to regard this prophet as himself the messenger of the coming one on whose behalf he had been commissioned to speak. This seems the more probable view, and it means that we cannot identify the author by name; whether any identification by way of the type of material in the collection is possible will be considered below.

Date

Just as there is a consensus concerning authorship, so also a generally agreed dating has emerged: the first half of the fifth century BC, after the establishment of the Second Temple in 515 and before the reforms of Nehemiah began about 445. (If the traditional dating of Ezra, 458, is accepted, this would make the conventional dating of Malachi still more precise.) The grounds for this judgment are mainly twofold: first the reference to the 'governor' (1.8) clearly implies that the *peḥâ* appointed by the Persian authorities, rather than a native king, is in a position of responsibility, and this implies the Second rather than the First Temple. (The word *peḥâ*, governor, is that used of Zerubbabel in Haggai and also of Nehemiah [Neh. 5.14; 12.26].) Secondly, it is commonly held that a more precise identification within the Persian period can be made on the basis of the various abuses listed in Malachi: the implication is that the reforms of Ezra and Nehemiah had not yet taken place. This is thought to point to a period after the first enthusiasm for temple-building had worn off and before the reforms which led to a purification of the cultus. Sometimes the attempt is made to provide external support for this dating by reference to the history of Edom: at some uncertain date the Edomites established themselves in the Negeb, south of Judah, as a result of Nabataean pressure in their traditional homelands, and it is argued that this is reflected in the condemnation of Edom in Mal. 1.2-6.

This matter of dating in fact raises rather greater problems of method than might appear at first sight. As has been said, the majority of commentators regard the indications that have been noted as sufficient evidence for a fairly precise date to be proposed, but there are others who are much more cautious. Ackroyd, for example, in a discussion of the history of Israel at this period, says that 'the light supposedly shed by the book of Malachi on some moment within this period is very meagre; ... the evidence on which

Malachi is dated is in fact very slender' ('The History of Israel in the Exilic and Post-Exilic Periods', in G.W. Anderson (ed.), *Tradition and Interpretation*, 332).

The reasons for this divergence of view are basically twofold, and they are worthy of attention because in principle they also apply to a great deal of other prophetic material. First, it is far from certain whether the references to Edom should be taken as historical ('mere history' as Ackroyd calls it, perhaps somewhat quaintly in an article devoted to historical problems [see above]) or whether Edom represents here *the* typical enemy. Edom is in fact portrayed as such in a great variety of material in the Old Testament, from the Jacob-Esau stories in Genesis through Amos, Jeremiah and Obadiah down to Malachi, but it would be precarious indeed to attempt a precise historical reconstruction of the underlying situations behind each of these prophetic condemnations. In other words, Mal. 1.2-6 may reflect a literary continuum as much as an historical comment.

Secondly, we need to be aware of the gaps in our historical knowledge. In the Second Temple period in particular these are far too great for detailed reconstruction to be legitimate. The books of Ezra and Nehemiah each make the claim on behalf of their hero that real reform was carried out under his guidance; but we have no means of knowing how widespread or lasting such reforms may have been. What is more, it would be surprising indeed if even after a reform had been carried out there had not still been some malpractice remaining which could legitimately be identified and condemned. This point is an important one for the study of the prophetic books generally. We are accustomed to date them by reference to the opening verses. In fact, as has been widely recognized in recent years, these are editorial additions, and cannot always be relied upon as a guide to the dating of the material which follows. Living prophetic traditions cannot be pinned down to precise points in time.

Our conclusion with regard to dating must therefore be that Malachi is to be placed within the Persian period, some time between 515 and 330 BC; but that greater precision than that is scarcely available.

Deuteronomistic Links in Malachi

One other preliminary point deserves consideration before we look at the main features of Malachi's message. This concerns the attempt to determine the nature of the connection between Malachi and the Deuteronomistic writings. These writings have been the subject of a great deal of attention in recent years, but the links with Malachi had been noted long before this particular upsurge of interest. Thus, J.M.P. Smith, the commentator on Malachi in the ICC volume of 1912, noted in particular that the reference to the priests as bound by the covenant with Levi (2.4, 8) and the use of such expressions as 'the law of my servant Moses', 'Horeb' and 'all Israel' (4.4) all point to links with Deuteronomy rather than with the Priestly Code. This may have some bearing on date, in so far as reference to an Aaronic priesthood and to the holy mountain as Sinai increasingly became the norm; but a greater significance of this kind of usage lies in the fact that Malachi appears to have been attempting to apply the particular emphases of the Deuteronomists in the circumstances of his own day. If this is so, it would be an interesting converse of the Deuteronomistic editing of earlier prophets. There the Deuteronomists were shaping the prophetic words in the light of their own perception of God's dealings with his people; here a prophet's own words are being shaped by the need to make the Deuteronomists' appeal to Israel relevant to changing circumstances.

It is in this light that a further link with the Deuteronomists can best be understood. As R.L. Smith rightly points out (Commentary, 300) it is not simply through certain *words* that links with Deuteronomy can be traced: the *themes* of Malachi are also characteristically those of Deuteronomy. Smith refers in particular to 'love' 'fear' and 'faithfulness' as being especially noteworthy in this regard. This comment forms a natural link to a consideration of the main aspects of Malachi's message.

Form and Message

These two subjects are best taken together, for the unusual form of Malachi seems to have been deliberately adapted to the substance of the message he has to give. The form is unique in a prophetic book in that it consists of an exchange of a series of questions and answers between the prophet and his hearers. This form is found elsewhere as one element in a prophetic collection (e.g. in Hag. 1.4ff.; 2.3ff.), but nowhere else is it carried through as here so as to cover virtually the whole book, and nowhere else are the supposed answers of those accused set out in the detail given in Malachi, which is interspersed with phrases such as 'You say', introducing the answers to the prophetic accusations. Such a form probably has a legal background, with charges being made, answers being put forward, and these in their turn being dismissed as inadequate. Such a form at once indicates that a large part of the message will be one of condemnation, as is also the case with the pre-exilic prophets when legal terms are used. In the study of the pre-exilic prophets there has been much discussion about the possible use by them of a 'controversy' or 'lawsuit' pattern (*rîb*) as a literary genre (see, for example, K. Nielsen, *Yahweh as Prosecutor and Judge*, Sheffield: JSOT Press, 1978). Malachi has some elements in common with this proposed pattern, particularly in the accusatory material of 1.6–2.9, but it would be impossible to reconstruct anything like a complete 'lawsuit' from Malachi.

There is another and perhaps more important respect in which the condemnations in Malachi differ from those found in the pre-exilic prophets. The words of the earlier prophets appear to have been addressed to the whole community: to a nation involved in all the multifarious activities of a nation-state. Among those activities religion will have been more prominent than would be usual today, but it was not the only concern. With Malachi things have changed: he is overwhelmingly concerned with religious matters, with the priesthood and the temple, and with the proper way in which God should be worshipped. However, Malachi is entirely at one with his predecessors and a genuine heir of the prophetic tradition in his recognition of the responsibility laid on the religious leaders, on whom he is very much more severe than on the community at large. The priests in particular are harshly condemned (1.6–2.9).

Yet this condemnation is not the only impression left by the book of Malachi. In a way without exact parallel elsewhere in the prophets we find in the often very severe words of judgment expressions which bring out a strongly positive aspect of God's power. Thus in 1.5 the initial condemnation of Edom, which is in some respects very harsh and negative, reaches its climax in an assertion of Yahweh's supranational power. More remarkable, and much discussed, is 1.11, rightly described by R.L. Smith (312) as 'one of the most difficult verses in the OT to interpret'. Smith goes on to outline no fewer than five different lines of interpretation which have been suggested. Among these we may note the importance that this verse has had in

Christian liturgical history, the 'pure offering' to which it refers
being interpreted as being in some way 'fulfilled' by the Christian
eucharist. However that may be, this can scarcely be considered
probable as the original intention of the prophet. Nor is it likely that
the suggestion, widely propounded earlier this century, that any
sincere pagan worship is here regarded as acceptable represents the
intended thrust of this verse. (For a critique of this view see
Baldwin's Commentary, 227-29, and her article, 'Malachi 1.11 and
the Worship of the Nations in the Old Testament'.) This kind of
universalism is not characteristic of the Old Testament. Another
possibility is that the reference here might be to the Jews living away
from Jerusalem, in the Diaspora. This is an interpretation which was
widely accepted among later Jewish commentators; it has also been
defended recently by J. Blenkinsopp (*A History of Prophecy in Israel*,
240f.). But perhaps the most likely interpretation is provided by the
clue noted by Mason, that the phrase 'from the rising of the sun to its
setting' is virtually identical with Ps. 50.1b. In that Psalm, as in this
verse, the Lord's universal power is proclaimed, and the efficacy of
animal sacrifice rejected. In Mal. 1.11 too the sacrifices referred to
are not those of animals. It seems therefore that we may legitimately
see here a proclamation of the Lord's universal power, perhaps set
over against excessive claims made on behalf of the sacrificial system
of the Jerusalem temple as being the only assured way to divine
favour. If so, Malachi will have anticipated some of the bitter
disputes concerning the status of the Jerusalem cult which
characterized post-biblical Judaism and can still be traced in the New
Testament.

There are other individual verses in Malachi whose significance is
disputed (cf. in particular the very varied interpretations offered by
the commentators on 2.10-16); but the other main point of
importance relates to the appendices which form the last few verses
of the book (4.4-6). The last main section of the book consists of
3.13–4.3, with its characteristic warning of judgment for the wicked;
but there follow three verses which clearly stand somewhat apart.
Almost all scholars consider these verses to be later additions: the
only recent exception to this judgment is that of Baldwin, who
regards their style and continued ethical emphasis to be sufficiently
in keeping with what precedes to point to Malachi as their probable
author (Commentary, 251). In fact the very sharp difference in form
makes it more likely that these verses are a later addition, though the

continued Deuteronomistic links (e.g. the use of 'Horeb' in 4.4) certainly supply a measure of continuity with what has preceded. The particular points of significance in these verses, however, are those which distinguish them from the main body of Malachi. In particular we may note the following:

1. The reference in 4.4 to 'the law of my servant Moses, the statutes and ordinances that I commanded him' is strongly, and surely intentionally, reminiscent of Deuteronomy. That book too is in form a looking-back upon what God had done for his people at Horeb, with the intention of emphasizing the continued importance of the commands made there for a later generation. Here in Malachi at an even later time than Deuteronomy we find it strongly emphasized that those laws are still operative despite all the changes that have taken place in the life of the commnity.

2. The form of this reference strongly suggests that the 'law' (Heb. *tôrâ*) has now reached a fixed and effectively final shape: it can in effect be appealed to as 'Scripture'. The community that is to 'remember' this law is now the community which is bound to God by a Holy Book as well as by the sacrifices of the temple. And it is now 'Israel' in the sense of a religious grouping, not of a nation-state.

3. The second appendix (4.5-6) has little direct connection with the first and may come from another hand. It is in effect an explanatory gloss on 3.1, elaborating on the identity of the promised messenger, the link between the two passages perhaps being provided by the reference to 'Horeb', the name given to Sinai in Deuteronomy and the mountain to which Elijah fled according to 1 Kings 19. The first appendix looked back; this one looks forward. It is the first example known to us of the working out of a role for Elijah in God's future plans. The Elijah stories in 1–2 Kings already witness to an elaboration of traditions about him, and that process continued in post-biblical Judaism. The story in 2 Kings 2 of Elijah's departure in a whirlwind probably facilitated this growth of later legend: he was pictured as being with God, awaiting his further instructions, rather than as having died a normal death.

In two important ways these verses are taken up in the New Testament. First, in the vision in the story of Jesus' transfiguration, Moses and Elijah are linked together (Mark 9.4f. and parallels); secondly, the question whether John the Baptist fits the role here attributed to Elijah is reflected in both Matthew and John. Matthew represents a tradition which appears to identify John with Elijah

(Matt. 11.14); in John this is clearly denied (John 1.21). The resolution of this discrepancy must be left to New Testament students.

There is a fourth point which could be made about this appended section of Malachi. It relates to the way in which it rounds off the whole prophetic collection. But that is a matter perhaps better left to our concluding chapter, when we shall look briefly at ways of approaching the books here under scrutiny other than the usual historical-critical method.

Further Reading

The commentaries by Baldwin, Jones, Mason and R.L. Smith listed and briefly discussed at the end of Chapter 4 also extend to Malachi. The Malachi commentary in *IB* is by R.C. Dentan, and that in ICC by J.M.P. Smith. (Each of these is in the same volume as the commentaries by D.W. Thomas and H.G. Mitchell listed earlier.)

Other relevant studies:

J.G. Baldwin, 'Malachi 1.11 and the Worship of the Nations in the Old Testament', *Tyndale Bulletin* 23 (1972), 117-24.
J. Blenkinsopp, *A History of Prophecy in Israel*, 240-42.
J. Swetnam, 'Malachi 1.11: an Interpretation', *CBQ* 31 (1969), 200-209 (on the limitations of earlier Catholic interpretations of this verse, and the likelihood of its referring to the Diaspora).

9

THE
LARGER
CONTEXT

IN OUR STUDY of Zechariah 1–14 we saw how various episodes in those chapters were understood by the New Testament writers as pointing forward to the life and work of Jesus. Such a method of interpreting the prophetic literature was normal in the church for many centuries; this literature was seen as something which pointed beyond itself towards a fulfilment, either in Jesus or in a consummation at the end of the world. This mode of understanding is by no means defunct—Zech. 9.9-12, for example, remains in many lectionaries the standard reading for Palm Sunday—but it is now often thought to share a somewhat uneasy co-existence with other more 'scientific' or 'scholarly' types of understanding.

Of these 'scholarly' approaches it is the historical-critical method which has overwhelmingly dominated research. The prophets are assigned to their original life-setting: we speak of 'eighth-century prophets' or 'sixth-century prophets', and anything that does not come from that original setting is often regarded as secondary and of inferior value. Most Introductions to the Old Testament devote a good deal of attention to isolating the original message of the prophet after whom a book is named. Even more revealingly, they usually treat the prophets in what is judged to be their historical order rather than in the order in which the tradition has handed down their oracles to us.

To take a typical example, one of the best modern introductions, that by J.A. Soggin, divides its treatment of the prophets into two sections, Pre-Exilic and Exilic/Post-Exilic, and works through each book in its supposed chronological order, beginning with Amos, and ending Haggai–Zechariah–Trito Isaiah–Obadiah–Malachi–Deutero-Zechariah–Joel–Jonah. It will be noted straightaway that this order departs drastically from the order in which the books appear in our Bibles. It is also assumed that it is possible to identify the date of the prophet as an individual with the date of the book incorporating his oracles. For example, Amos is simply taken to be a prophet of doom. This is no doubt true with regard to the message of the individual prophet, but the complete book of Amos, with its hopeful ending, gives a very different picture. Beyond the inevitable disaster there is a confident expectation of salvation:

> 'I will restore the fortune of my people Israel,
> > and they shall rebuild the ruined cities and inhabit them'
> > (Amos 9.14).

This is the form that has come down to us; what once underlay it as the actual words of the prophet must remain a matter of speculation.

These comments are not in any sense intended to suggest that the historical-critical method is wrong, or even misguided: if it were, for a start much of what has been written here would need to be set aside. But this is not the only possible or legitimate method of studying the prophets, or individual parts of the collection; and two other approaches may be noted in conclusion which help to highlight certain other aspects of the prophetic collections here studied. (A third possibility will not here be pursued: that of 'close reading' in the literary-critical sense. Such an approach can be immensely rewarding in narrative texts, or with a poetic structure such as the book of Job, but is less obviously helpful in an analysis of prophetic oracular material.) The two concerns that will be taken up are the final form of the books here being studied, and their place within the canon, particularly within the Book of the Twelve.

Some consideration has already been given (Chapter 3) to the nature of the editorial process which Haggai and Zechariah 1–8 have undergone, and we have also noted links between Zechariah 9–14 and Malachi. But the tradition has handed down a threefold division (Hag., Zech., Mal.) rather than this twofold one. There is likely to be a sense in which the final form of each book has a particular thrust, a particular shape given to the prophetic material contained within it. Since we do not know to whom the final form of the book of Haggai, or Zechariah, or Malachi, was addressed or the particular historical or social circumstances of the community, any reconstruction has to be speculative. Even so, some pointers can be noted.

For *Haggai*, it is clear that the demand for the rebuilding of the temple was no longer relevant when the book reached its final form. But those to whom it was addressed in that form still needed to be reminded of the importance of the role that the temple had played in their corporate life: just as the community had built the temple, so the temple had built up the community. Each contributed to the other's well-being, and must continue to do so, for only in that way could the full manifestation of God's presence with his people find its real context. Then, and only then, the community was being told, could the expectations of Hag. 2.6-9 reach fulfilment. 'The latter splendour of this house shall be greater than the former, says the LORD of hosts; and in this place I will give prosperity, says the LORD of hosts.'

In *Zechariah* we have the phenomenon of two blocks of material of different origins which have been juxtaposed to form one book. What effect would this have had? It seems likely that the characteristic feature combining the two parts will have been the visionary aspect which is so prominent in each. Zechariah is a visionary book, both in the sense that the prophetic message is conveyed to a large extent through visions rather than purely through verbal messages, and in the sense that it stretches out toward a vision of the future. The 'that day' of Zechariah is not simply the day of punishment found in so many earlier prophetic passages or the day of the reign of Darius as in 1.7; it is a day to which the people can look forward, when the limitations and frustrations of their existing situation will have been transformed. Typical is 14.16: 'Then every one that survives of all the nations that have come against Jerusalem shall go up year after year to worship the King, the LORD of hosts, and to keep the feast of booths'. Such a promise is addressed to a community for whom the proper observance of the round of festivals is important; it is also couched in 'this-worldly' terms. There is here nothing of the complete overthrow of the existing world order which came to characterize the later apocalypses.

One other point may probably be claimed as a message to be gleaned from the complete book of Zechariah. Throughout there is the concern to stress that earlier prophetic words are still valid, that their working-out has not been overlooked. Prophets are now figures from the past (1.4-6), and those who claim such status in the present are to be distrusted (13.2-6); the words of those past prophets were, for the community to which Zechariah was addressed, threats and promises whose exact implications God would in his own good time reveal. This is still a long way from the understanding of prophecy to be found in the Dead Sea Scrolls or the New Testament; it is nonetheless a significant step in the direction of such an understanding.

In *Malachi* also an important aspect of the message of the final form of the book is this same process of making contemporary the words and lives of God's earlier messengers. The people are Israel (1.1), identified with Jacob over against Edom/Esau (1.2-5), in a way that only makes sense if the Genesis stories are kept in mind. Israel has to remain loyal to the statutes and ordinances given through Moses at Horeb (4.4), laws which the people's present behaviour is contravening. Only when that has been corrected will the future be open, and the community be ready to receive the promised Elijah, who will finally set right the structures of the community before the day of the LORD comes (4.5f.).

These verses bring the book of Malachi to an end; they also form the conclusion of the 'Book of the Twelve', the Minor Prophets. Modern critical scholarship, with its mainly historical concerns, has almost entirely ignored any sense of a 'Book' in studying the Minor Prophets. The twelve units are studied individually, usually in an assumed historical order, not of the books but of the individuals after whom they are named; and any sense of order and continuity within the collection is soon lost by this process. (How widespread this assumption of twelve discrete units has become may be illustrated by looking at church lectionaries, not normally regarded as bastions of critical methods. In the Church of England, for example, whereas the Cranmer lectionary of the Book of Common Prayer provided for the Book of the Twelve to be read straight through, all twentieth-century revisions down to the Alternative Service Book of 1980 distribute the readings from the Minor Prophets through different parts of the year.)

The legitimacy of this division for many purposes is not in question, but it is valuable to observe the way in which the Book of the Twelve is a genuine book. This is often best seen by the way in which references from one individual collection are picked up in the next: compare for example Joel 3.16 with the following book, Amos

1.2, or the way in which Amos's final words relating to Edom provide the theme of the next collection, Obadiah. In our present study we have seen links between Haggai and Zechariah and between Zechariah and Malachi, and it is surely also legitimate to see Haggai's concern for the proper ordering of the temple as owing something to the hymnic passage in Zephaniah which immediately precedes it, promising a great festival in the temple on Zion when God himself would be in the midst of his people (Zeph. 3.17f.). In just the same way Haggai's community could look forward to God's presence with them when all his commands had been carried out (Hag. 2.5).

The scholar who has done most to draw our attention to the final or canonical shape of the biblical writings is B.S. Childs, and it is surprising that his *Introduction to the Old Testament as Scripture* does not contain a section discussing the Book of the Twelve as a unity. The Book of the Twelve is clearly not an authorial unity, and the different sections come from widely different settings; yet it is equally clearly not a collection of prophetic oracles juxtaposed at random. When we look at it as a unity it soon becomes apparent how certain themes develop within the book as a whole. Thus, the foreign enemy, so dire and threatening in Hosea, Joel and Amos, has been transformed by the end of the book (notice the importance of Jonah here!) into a power with whom Israel can live at peace (the references to Persian rule in Haggai and Zechariah) or into people who would one day join in worship of God in Jerusalem. Similarly we can see a development in attitude towards Israel's own religious practice: the condemnations of the earlier sections lead to drastic punishment and then to purification, though even at the very end (Malachi) warnings of corruption still need to be issued.

It would be absurd to look for a 'story-line' in the Book of the Twelve; it is an anthology, yet not a random gathering of diverse pieces. Just as we should beware of discussing the meaning of one particular passage without looking at its larger context within the prophetic book in which we find it, so it is legitimate and at times illuminating to look at a still larger context: that of the Book of the Twelve as a whole. This will enable us to see something of the way in which the complete and intricate pattern of the Hebrew Bible developed and was understood. Without making any exaggerated claims that Haggai, Zechariah and Malachi are the most important collections in our Bible, it may be affirmed that they afford a valuable insight both into the historical development of the Jewish community in the Second Temple period and into the literary process of drawing together in final form the sacred traditions of that community.

Further Reading

B.S. Childs, *Introduction to the Old Testament as Scripture*, 467-70, 476-85, 491-97 (on the 'canonical shape' of our three prophetic books).

R.J. Coggins, 'The Literary Approach to the Bible', *ExpT* 96 (1984), 9-14 (an introduction to some of the methods and problems of newer literary approaches).

R.E. Clements, 'Patterns in the Prophetic Canon', in G.W. Coats and B.O. Long (eds.), *Canon and Authority*, Philadelphia: Fortress Press, 1977, 42-55.

J.F.A. Sawyer, 'A Change of Emphasis in the Study of the Prophets', in Coggins, Phillips and Knibb (eds.), *Israel's Prophetic Tradition*, Cambridge, 1982, 233-49.

J.F.A. Sawyer, *From Moses to Patmos*, London: SPCK, 1977, especially ch. 6, 'Prophets and their Interpreters', 95-118.

INDEXES

INDEX OF BIBLICAL REFERENCES

INDEX OF AUTHORS